DEPARTMENT OF ENGLISH LOCAL HISTORY

OCCASIONAL PAPERS

Second Series

EDITED BY ALAN EVERITT

Number 1

Change in the Provinces: the Seventeenth Century

by

ALAN EVERITT

M.A., Ph.D., F.R.Hist.S.

Hatton Professor of English Local History
in the University of Leicester

LEICESTER UNIVERSITY PRESS

1969

First published in 1969 by
Leicester University Press

Distributed in North America by
Humanities Press Inc., New York

Copyright © Alan Everitt 1969

Set in Monotype Baskerville
Printed in Great Britain at
The Broadwater Press, Welwyn Garden City, Hertfordshire

SBN 7185 2022 X

CONTENTS

PREFACE   page 4

INTRODUCTION   5

I   THE ANATOMY OF PROVINCIAL LIFE   5
Diversity
Insularity
Continuity

II   THE ELEMENTS OF CONSERVATISM   15
The Distribution of Wealth
Regional Cultures and Capitals
Kinship and Cousinage
Insecurity and Authority

III   THE ELEMENTS OF CHANGE   35
Dependent Communities
The New Gentry
The Wayfaring Community
The Professions and the Pseudo-Gentry

IV   THE PROVINCES AND THE NATION   46

APPENDIX: THE DISTRIBUTION OF WEALTH IN ENGLAND   53
Table I   The Monthly Assessments, 1648–60
Table II   The Hearth Tax Assessments, 1662
Table III(a)   The Wealth of Yorkshire Families, *c.* 1640
Table III(b) The Wealth of Kentish Families, *c.* 1640

PREFACE

THIS paper is the first in a new series of Occasional Papers to be issued at intervals by the Department of English Local History in the University of Leicester, and published by Leicester University Press. The ideals and aims of the Department are now well known and need no recapitulation here. They were defined by Professor H. P. R. Finberg in 1954, in the initial paper of the original series, *The Local Historian and his Theme*. The present series will, in general, follow broadly similar lines to the first.

The aim of the Leicester school of Local History is a twofold one. First, it sets out to study the origins, the growth, and (where appropriate) the decay of some particular local community, or the development of some selected local landscape, so far as that landscape has been shaped by human forces. Secondly, it endeavours to discover, elucidate, and teach others to apply the general principles, patterns, or historical 'laws' that appear to govern, in varying guises and degrees, the history of the local community or the local landscape in England. The scope of the Occasional Papers therefore includes both the study of particular local communities in detail, such as Northampton or Coventry, and the study of more general developments in provincial society, such as are covered by the present paper.

INTRODUCTION

THE life of a provincial community, Balzac once remarked, is certainly not in the main current of the age. Until recent years probably most English historians would have agreed with the great Parisian novelist. Gradually, however, and for diverse reasons which there is happily no need to elucidate here, a certain change has been coming over English historiography. We are not all now so convinced of the dogma that everything must be viewed in its relationship to London and Westminster. Perhaps the truth is that many of us are not particularly interested in the main current of the age. Or perhaps, as the present writer thinks, there were many diverse and conflicting currents in the history of the seventeenth century, most of which neither originated in nor disembogued at the metropolis. There are, after all, other rivers in the world than the Thames and the Tyburn. And to mankind at large the human comedy as a whole, in all its infinite variety, is probably a more absorbing spectacle than the often rather tiresome political dramas enacted at Westminster.

This paper touches upon the *comédie humaine* as it was played out in the English provinces alone.[1] The aim has been to elucidate some of the conservative elements in the so-called 'crisis of the seventeenth century' as well as the elements of change. To write of the crisis in the space of a single paper is, perhaps, to fly in the face of providence, or at least some of one's most respected colleagues. In mercy both to readers and to the author merely a few themes have been singled out from among many in the pattern of provincial society, without making any claim that these isolated threads constituted the whole fabric. In the present state of our knowledge such a claim would be mere arrogance. English provincial society was so diverse, so complex, that we need to understand far more about its fascinating diversity before we can advance any procrustean theories about the nature of the crisis itself.

I THE ANATOMY OF PROVINCIAL LIFE

STILL, there are certain generalizations that can be made about provincial England in the seventeenth century. To begin with, three may be made. These may not seem at first sight the predominant characteris-

[1] The original draft of this paper was read at Birmingham University, in October 1967, in a series of public lectures on 'Crisis in England, 1603–1660'. Since then it has been expanded and largely rewritten in its present form.

tics of the time. But they are selected deliberately because, if it is necessary to devise any theory to explain the crisis, we must devise one which will explain the 'conservative reaction' of 1659–60 as well as the revolutionary developments of 1640–9. All too often the events of 1659–60 have in the past been hurried over with indecent celerity, or explained away as an inevitable reaction, a strange aberration of human nature, or a cunning plot between Cavaliers and ecclesiastics. No doubt there is a certain amount of truth in all these explanations; for human nature, there is reason to think, was almost as self-seeking and perverse in the 1660s as it is in the 1960s. Quite clearly, however, they do not afford an adequate explanation of the Restoration period, or a convincing sequel to the events of 1640–9.

Diversity

The first generalization that must be made is simply the importance of this *diversity* in provincial life. There were 40 county communities, more than 700 urban communities, and 9,000 rural parishes in England, all distinct from one another, all consciously separate, and many surprisingly different.[1] There were great differences in the social structure, the political temper, and the economic fortunes even of two adjacent counties in this period, Leicestershire and Northamptonshire, and their two county towns.[2] The former shire was governed by the antique power, not to say torn apart by the personal feuds, of two rival families, the Greys at Bradgate Park and the Hastingses at Ashby de la Zouch. Behind these magnates, the country gentry aligned themselves in the Civil War in more or less meek submission. And the town of Leicester, incapable of decisive action itself, and trying to placate both sides, was sacked by Prince Rupert in consequence. It took the best part of a generation to recover from its economic disaster. Northamptonshire, by contrast, was firmly controlled from the outset by an impressive caucus of new, rich, decisive, and often puritan gentry, in alliance with the equally strong-minded puritans of the county town, so that borough and shire, despite royalist plundering, seem to have emerged in 1660 on the whole considerably augmented in prosperity. Certainly the town of Northampton benefited from the Civil War: for a series of orders placed with its shoemakers, for many thousands of pairs of shoes

[1] For the number of market towns in this period see my chapter, 'The Marketing of Agricultural Produce', in *The Agrarian History of England and Wales*, IV, 1500–1640, ed. Joan Thirsk, 1967, pp. 467–77.

[2] This paragraph is based principally on unpublished research, relating to the family and political history of the two counties, in contemporary tracts, newspapers, State Papers, borough records (Northampton and Leicester), and parish and county histories (principally Nichols's *Leicestershire* and Baker's and Bridges's *Northamptonshire*). It also rests on an analysis of the lists of county committeemen for 1642–60, printed in the acts of parliament in C. H. Firth and R. S. Rait, *Acts and Ordinances of the Interregnum, 1642–1660*, 1911. See also J. H. Plumb, 'Political History, 1530–1885', V.C.H., *Leics.*, II, pp. 109–18; J. F. Hollings, *Leicester during the Great Civil War*, 1840.

for the parliamentarian armies, provided the foundation of the great shoe-trade for which it is still noted.[1] No wonder Clarendon, while remarking that there were in Leicester many faithful hearts to the king, was provoked to say of Northampton that it would have shut its gates against His Majesty himself, as Hull had done, if he had appeared before it. Indeed the whole county of Northampton, he said, was "of very eminent disaffection to the king throughout the war."[2] Nor is there any wonder if, a generation later, the wealthy county town on the Nene, despite a disastrous fire in 1675, was described by John Evelyn as a place "that for the beauty of the buildings, especially the church and town-house, may compare with the neatest in Italy itself": whereas Leicester, still struggling to regain its prosperity, was dubbed "an old stinking town, situated upon a dull river".[3] The difference shows how fatal it is to try and please two people at once.

If two counties so close to one another and two towns so similar in size and function could be so unlike, it is certain there were greater differences between local communities in more distant parts of England. One of the features of seventeenth-century England was the sudden changes of scenery and society to be met with even within the same shire. Take the county of Kent.[4] The northern fringes of the county, bordering the Thames and the North Sea, were amongst the most fertile and highly cultivated in England. Yet this area of commercialized farming, oriented primarily to the London and overseas markets, was in fact only a narrow ribbon of country, a fringe four or five miles wide, between the downs and the sea. It was the area Stuart travellers saw as they travelled down the Dover road, and they described it in detail. But what they rarely saw were the more extensive tracts of country to the south: the densely wooded downlands, the largely sterile quarry-hills beyond, and the vast area of the Weald reaching away into Sussex: tracts of country then surprisingly remote, especially in winter, to all but their native inhabitants. Indeed, in the

---

[1] V.C.H., *Northants.*, II, pp. 319 sq.; J. C. Cox, ed., *The Records of the Borough of Northampton*, 1898, II, pp. 294–5.

[2] Clarendon, *The History of the Rebellion and Civil Wars in England*, ed. W. D. Macray, 1888, II, p. 241; IV, pp. 39, 212. Clarendon also says Leicester was "disaffected generally" to the king; but this is hardly borne out by his own remarks elsewhere or by the general tenor of contemporary evidence in tracts, journals, and newsletters. For the opinions of Northamptonshire people generally, see also p. 38 *infra*.

[3] John Evelyn, *Diary*, *sub* 23 August 1688 (cf. also his remarks on Leicester and Leicestershire *sub* 9 August 1654); H.M.C., *Portland*, II, p. 308. At Northampton, four-fifths of the town had been destroyed by fire in 1675. The rapidity and modernity of its rebuilding was a further sign of its wealth.

[4] This paragraph is based on research in Kentish family and agrarian history in this period: cf. my *The Community of Kent and the Great Rebellion, 1640–60*, chapter II. The extent of peasant husbandry in the county is shown in the probably unrivalled collection of Kentish probate inventories. These have been estimated at 40,000 for the diocese of Canterbury alone (1523–1857, the great bulk before the late eighteenth century). In rural parishes the vast majority, as in other counties, relate to yeomen and husbandmen.

forests around Sevenoaks and Dorking, within 25 miles of St Paul's, Tudor and Stuart people were still hunting wild boars and the native red deer, in valleys where their modern descendants exercise their poodles.[1] In a country like England, where contrasts of scenery and society occurred within so short a distance of each other, it is not surprising if the local reactions to the Civil War were often confused, mercurial, and at first sight incomprehensible.

Insularity

The second generalization about provincial society follows rather obviously from these conditions: and that is the insularity of local communities and the tenacity of local attachments. Not that any English community by this date was wholly insular. Few, if any, were entirely self-supporting. The existence of 750 market-centres is one indication, one among many, of the extent of inland trade in this period, and of the dependence of country people as well as townsmen upon the products of other districts than their own. Probably we are all learning, moreover, that there was more mobility among the rural population than perhaps used to be supposed. But still, local attachments remained strong. Even among those who left their native villages this was true. Many who migrated to other parts of England left money to their old towns to endow almshouses, to feed the poor, or to rebuild a market house.[2] Some provided bibles and books of piety for the children of those they had grown up with years ago. When Dr John Favour, the Elizabethan vicar of Halifax, came to make his will after many years in the north of England, his thoughts reverted, with a characteristic homing instinct, to the south-country town he had known in his youth. He bequeathed a bible to the people of Southampton, he said, "out of the love he beareth unto his dear country [of Hampshire] . . . that it may be chained to a desk in the council chamber of the Audit House for the edification of those that shall read therein."[3]

If such attachments remained powerful among those who left their birthplace, they were naturally stronger among the majority who remained behind. Perhaps we unconsciously exaggerate the extent to which the inhabitants of

[1] Daniel Defoe, *A Tour through England and Wales*, Everyman edn, 1959, I, p. 154; W. Jerrold, *Highways and Byways in Kent*, 1914 edn, p. 322; E. W. Brayley, *Beauties of England and Wales*, VIII (Kent), p. 1326.

[2] Bequests by former inhabitants for the rebuilding of market-houses are sometimes referred to in the Exchequer Special Commissions and Depositions regarding markets and market-tolls in the Public Record Office (classes E.134 and E.178).

[3] Quoted in A. L. Rowse, *The England of Elizabeth*, 1964 edn, p. 431. The same instincts moved Sir Edward Dering, when stricken with a fatal disease in 1644, to return from Oxford to his native Kent—to die, he said, where to him the air was "the sweetest air in the land" (*A Discourse of Proper Sacrifice*, 1644).

any one local community—village, town, or county—were usually aware of what went on in other parts of the country. True, the court peers and a small proportion of major gentry who had houses in London, perhaps at the most one-tenth of all the gentry, were reasonably well-informed, if only intermittently, of events in London. And several hundred MPs were, one supposes, not wholly ignorant: while parliament was sitting they formed, indeed, important channels of news to their local constituents.[1] But for the majority of the population below this level, for the whole urban and agrarian basis of provincial society, contacts with other parts of the kingdom, though of increasing importance, were still spasmodic and occasional rather than normal. For this reason their reactions were frequently ill-informed and unpredictable.[2] To each successive government they were a danger, if not an insoluble problem. For most of the people, most of the time, political matters scarcely existed. How could they? There was no radio or television; there were no provincial newspapers. Away from the towns and the main roads, especially in the forest areas of England, such as Rockingham Forest in Northamptonshire or the Weald of Sussex and Kent, problems of transport, and often flooded roads, isolated ordinary people from the outside world for weeks at a time.

There are many little touches in family letters, diaries, lawsuits, tracts, and journals in this period that bring home the extent to which local communities lived, or wished to live, a life of their own apart from the mainstream of national politics. One finds, for example, that in speaking of their 'country' people in Yorkshire, Norfolk, and Kent did not mean England but their own county. In speaking of 'the western parts' Kentish folk rarely meant what we mean by the phrase, but merely west Kent. True, they did individualize some other English counties, either because of their trading contacts with them, as with Devon, Hampshire, and Norfolk, or because of their proximity, as in the case of Essex and Sussex. "The Sussex men", some of them characteristically remarked at Rochester in 1640, "are especially ungovernable." The rebels from the London suburbs who essayed to join them in the Rising of 1648 they described as "those mad souls".[3] The rest of England, including all the counties north of the Thames, they denominated indiscriminately as 'the Sheeres'.

Equally strange, perhaps, to an age of illustrated newspapers and television, is the fact that most ordinary people in Kent had no idea of what Charles I and the Prince of Wales looked like. They had never seen them, or probably even a

[1] Cf. Madeline Jones, *The Political History of the Parliamentary Boroughs of Kent, 1642–62*, London Ph.D. thesis, 1967, pp. 289–90; Everitt, *Community of Kent*, p. 226. In Yorkshire, Dr J. T. Cliffe tells me, it is doubtful if more than twenty heads of households had London houses in 1642.

[2] Cf. H. G. Tibbutt, ed., *The Letter Books of Sir Samuel Luke*, 1963, pp. 292, 304, for the effect of rumour on reactions in Northants. and Bucks. in 1645.

[3] *Cal. State Papers Dom.*, 1640, pp. 539–40; Everitt, *Community of Kent*, p. 252.

picture of them. When, in 1648, a penniless and fair-haired imposter landed at Sandwich and announced himself as the Prince of Wales, the unsuspecting townsmen flocked to kiss his hand, the wives of the burgesses brought out their silks and satins to make clothes for him, and the corporation lodged him in state and gave him a public banquet in the Guildhall. Not for some days was a Kentish baronet who had once seen the genuine, swarthy prince at Court able, with lengthy proofs, to undeceive them.[1] And all this despite the fact that this town was supposedly ultra-puritan and anti-royalist in its sympathies. We may smile at the naïvety and ignorance of the people of Sandwich: but what we need to sense is that here was a world where life was simply not polarized between Cavalier and Roundhead. It was not chiefly occupied with politics at all, but with its own affairs of buying, selling, making love, marrying, bringing up a family, and with all those thousand little concerns that tied together the bonds of family life, formed the staple of conversation, and made a community like Sandwich so introverted. Yet the influence of such a town on politics was not altogether negligible. Sandwich returned two members to parliament, and at times of crisis its decisions could be locally decisive in east Kent.

There were a number of developments in 1640–60 which tended to increase this introversion of the local community. One was the creation of the parliamentarian county committees in 1642–3, which brought together the most powerful families of each shire in an independent body or institution, a sort of county-council-cum-county-parliament. Another was the widespread underground reaction in the fifties, in many towns and amongst most country gentry, against Cromwell's efforts to establish a more efficient administrative system by weakening these county committees, and centralizing their powers in the hands of the secretaries of state and the major-generals.[2] A third development that tended to increase the insularity of the local community was the fact that, owing to the reorganization, or perhaps one should say the disorganization, of the church, the corporations of many towns, such as Northampton, Sandwich, and Maidstone, acquired direct control over the salaries, the appointments, and in some degree the opinions of their local ministers.[3]

All the time, moreover, strengthening the family cohesion of the local gentry, was the fact that they continued to marry, by and large, amongst their neighbours. This topic indeed requires further research before it can be definitely stated as a universal truth. But in Leicestershire, Yorkshire, Suffolk, and Northamptonshire it seems to be generally true amongst most gentry below the

---

[1] Bodleian Library, Clarendon MS 31, f. 97; B.M., E.445.13; E.443.26; Matthew Carter, *A most True and Exact Relation of that as Honourable as Unfortunate Expedition of Kent, Essex, and Colchester*, 1650, pp. 42–6.

[2] Everitt, *Community of Kent*, pp. 286–301.   [3] Madeline Jones, *op. cit.*, pp. 449–54.

topmost level of country magnates.[1] In Sussex we have the word of Mrs Hutchinson, a native of the county, "that it had been such a continued custom for my ancestors to take wives at home, that there was scarce a family of any note in Sussex to which they were not by intermarriages nearly related". In Cheshire, said Thomas Fuller, the gentry "find it more profitable to match within their county than to bring a bride out of other shires", so that "they are all of an alliance." "Better wed over the mixen than over the moor" was one of the proverbs of the county. In Cornwall, as Defoe remarked about the turn of the century, the gentry rarely married outside the county, which gave rise to the proverb that "all the Cornish gentlemen are cousins".[2] In Kent a similar proverb was current and more than four-fifths of the squirearchy married into local families. Virtually all of them were related to one redoubtable matriarch, Mary Honywood, whose living descendants at the time of her death in 1620, aged 93, numbered 367 persons.[3] Mary Honywood has earned a well-merited place in the *Dictionary of National Biography*. Through her alone, quite apart from others, the community of the Kentish gentry had become a single great cousinage well before the time of the Civil War. Yet its society displayed only in a more extreme form the same features that obtained in other shires, including those of Midland England, where county boundaries offered less pronounced barriers.

It was conditions of this kind that led the royalist leader in Kent, Sir Thomas Peyton, to marry his daughter to the son of a local regicide, and his stepson to the daughter of a parliamentarian colonel, without any apparent sense of inconsistency.[4] Peyton was certainly not a stupid man; but neither was he a calculating hypocrite. Indeed, he was honest and generous to the point of quixotry. It was simply that for him and his neighbours the sense of loyalty to Charles I was crossed and criss-crossed by loyalty to family and locality. This could be illustrated in many ways: for example from the numerous popular ballads and epics of the time vaunting, nominally in the royal cause, the prow-

[1] These remarks are based on family genealogies in the Heralds' Visitations, county and parish histories, and the standard genealogical journals. For information regarding Yorkshire I am indebted to Dr J. T. Cliffe. The tendency to marry locally was in some counties increasing. In Northamptonshire it transformed the somewhat newly-planted county community of the Stuart era into a society where the sense of cohesion and exclusion, by the eighteenth century, was exceptionally pronounced.

[2] *Memoirs of Colonel Hutchinson*, Everyman edn, 1965, p. 7; Thomas Fuller, *The History of the Worthies of England*, ed. P. A. Nuttall, 1840, I, pp. 266–7; Daniel Defoe, *A Tour Through England and Wales*, Everyman edn, 1959, I, p. 234. Mrs Hutchinson's own mother, however, was not a native of Sussex. Of the Dorset gentry Defoe remarked that "they seem to have a mutual confidence in, and friendship with one another, as if they were all relations", *ibid.*, p. 216.

[3] Everitt, *Community of Kent*, pp. 36, 42–3, 328. As might be expected, the proportion who married locally varied greatly in different parts of the county: it was highest in central and east Kent.

[4] Everitt, *Community of Kent*, pp. 219–20.

ess and independence of the community of Kent.[1] As poetry these effusions are of course execrable; but in the history of the local community they are significant, and to the student of human nature they are often humorous and sometimes strangely pathetic. Men like Sir Thomas Peyton often read and sometimes wrote these poems, and they perpetuated a legend of invincibility in the county that did not die out till the nineteenth century. It even found an echo in a well-known sonnet of Wordsworth's, and later still in a three-decker novel.[2] Such men as Peyton would have wholly agreed with the later Kentish historian, Edward Hasted, when he told William Pitt in 1799 that he had written "the history of a county which stands foremost in the rank of all others, so deservedly proud of its pre-eminence in every respect, and so noted for its loyalty". But, like Edward Hasted, I myself "might dwell much longer on so pleasing a subject, which I reluctantly quit lest I should exceed the bounds of decency".[3]

Continuity

The third general characteristic of provincial society in the seventeenth century was its sense of continuity with the past. Obviously this statement needs qualification. The degree of continuity was much greater in some areas than in others, and the causes of social mobility more potent in some types of community than others. Yet we need to remember that the far-reaching changes in provincial society which occurred between, say, the Reformation and the Civil War took place, not in the space of a single generation, but over three or four. The difference was vital, for by the year 1640 it had given time for many new families to settle down and strike root in the local soil. Probably in no English county was the landed revolution of the period leading up to the Civil War so sudden and overwhelming as that which took place, for example, in southwestern Scotland between 1780 and 1820. Even in Northamptonshire, where the process of change was exceptionally rapid, it cannot be compared in its revolutionary effects to that which occurred in Galloway and Kirkcudbrightshire in the reign of George III. In the latter county, for instance, virtually none of the early-Victorian landed estates are traceable as distinct entities before

---

[1] A typical example was an epic, *Halesiados*, published in 1648 to celebrate the deeds of the popular young Cavalier leader of Kent, Edward Hales of Tunstall Place. A later effusion in a parallel tradition was a poem on 'Gavelkind'—of all improbable subjects of verse—part of which is printed in *The Kentish Travellers' Companion*, 1779.

[2] *The Royalist and the Republican: a Story of the Kentish Insurrection*, 1852. The defence of Maidstone against vast odds in 1648 became a kind of folk-myth of Kentish independence. It was in Wordsworth's mind when he wrote the sonnet 'Vanguard of liberty, ye Men of Kent!'

[3] These phrases come from the Dedication of 1799 inserted in the British Museum copy of Volume I of the first edition (1778) of Hasted's *History and Topographical Survey of the County of Kent*.

1750 or 1800. Most of them were wholly new agglomerations of farms or small-holdings, with no historical unity, and with an entirely new laird's house where no mansion had formerly existed.[1]

All of us, no doubt, have by now seen Professor Stone's monumental volume *The Crisis of the Aristocracy, 1558–1641*. Some of us may even have read it. He argues very persuasively that there were grave problems facing the aristocracy during that period. And of course one must grant his point. A crisis, however, which continued for no less than eighty-three years seems perhaps a rather strange phenomenon. It was, after all, as long a period as separates the age of Mr Gladstone from the age of Mr Harold Wilson. Certainly it is difficult to grant Professor Stone's contention that most of the greater provincial gentry, about 1640, were second- or third-generation *nouveaux riches*. To suppose that most English gentry had risen in so short a time as forty or fifty years from the ranks of husbandmen, through trade, or the law, or royal office, to the level of peers, baronets, or knights is altogether too simplified a view. When one studies the members of a county community as a whole, instead of taking selected examples of local gentry, one finds that families who had so risen—such as the Fanes, the Cecils, the Fermors, the Spencers, or the Vanes—were not really typical of the country gentry in general. We tend to notice them more because they were striking and dramatic in their rise to fortune. But far more characteristic of county society in general were, on one hand, those greater gentry who had risen gradually over the centuries from the freeholders or minor armigerous families of the Middle Ages and, on the other, those numerous squires who had risen from the ranks of local yeomen during the sixteenth century. In Kent these two groups together comprised more than 90 per cent of the 800–900 gentry families who formed the county community. In Leicestershire they probably formed nearly two-thirds, and in Suffolk about 60 per cent of the squirearchy. Even in Northamptonshire, where the Tudor landed revolution was remarkably complete, they appear to have comprised nearly half the 335 gentle families in the county in 1640.[2] Such families had risen considerably in

[1] Alan Everitt, 'Social Mobility in Early Modern England', *Past and Present*, No. 33, April 1966, pp. 72–3.

[2] These figures are not exactly comparable with those of gentry origins I have given elsewhere: cf. *Suffolk and the Great Rebellion*, Suffolk Records Society, III, 1960, p. 20; *Community of Kent*, pp. 36–7; *Past and Present*, No. 33, April 1966, pp. 60–4. In these latter accounts I was speaking of families strictly indigenous in origin to the county concerned. This seems to me the proper basis to adopt for the study of any particular county community. In the figures above, however, I am endeavouring to demonstrate the strength of broadly local and agrarian influences, rather than metropolitan, mercantile, legal, and official ones, in the origins of the provincial gentry as a whole. I have therefore included in the figures for each county, as stated above, those families who originated just across the boundary in neighbouring shires. In a small Midland county like Northamptonshire, as might be expected, many families had originated as yeomen, etc., in nearby parishes of Buckinghamshire, Warwickshire,

the social scale since 1500, of course. The change in their fortunes had certainly helped to redirect the course of both local and national history. But they cannot be regarded as *nouveaux riches* in the same revolutionary sense as the Vanes, Spencers, and Cecils. Their origins and interests were primarily local; their sphere was confined to the parish or county; their wealth was gradually built up and still basically agrarian; their ambition was rarely the Woolsack or the Court, but rather the justices' bench. Probably in most counties a powerful core of families like these continued to control society throughout the first half of the seventeenth century. On the whole they gradually absorbed the complete newcomers into their ranks without themselves suffering more than a partial metamorphosis. Year by year, in ones and twos, the newcomers continued to arrive; but they had to come to terms, usually by intermarriage, with an already established hierarchy.

If one studies the houses of these native, local families one finds that the story of gradual and organic growth was far more characteristic of these, too, than a complete reconstruction within, say, a single decade. The seventeenth-century manor houses of counties like Devon, Kent, and Suffolk are usually on medieval sites, and commonly they include an earlier house within their structure. Frequently, as at Great Maydeacon and Godinton in Kent, the homes of the Oxinden and Toke families, building was a more or less continuous process. The manor house and its farm buildings were added to bit by bit, year after year, and the work was financed from the modest annual surplus of the squire's farming and rents.[1] In Leicestershire and Northamptonshire also this pattern now seems to me more characteristic than I used to think it. The Tudor and

Oxfordshire, and Leicestershire. From the point of view of their historical roots and connexions, these must obviously be reckoned as local and agrarian rather than as *nouveaux riches* in the same sense as the Fanes at Apethorpe, the Cecils at Burghley, or the Cartwrights at Aynho. Absolute accuracy cannot be claimed for the figures in the text. For relatively few families does adequate documentary evidence survive to compile a complete and detailed history. But in practice enough genealogical evidence usually exists to distinguish, broadly speaking, between families of predominantly 'metropolitan-mercantile-official' origin and those with mainly 'local-agrarian' roots. This seems to me the significant distinction in the present context. Provided one sufficiently familiarizes oneself with the county community as a whole, and the history of each family, the two species are not as a rule difficult to distinguish. There are always the problem families, of course, that do not fit exactly into either category. In the counties cited above I have not found that they affect the figures by more than 4 or 5 per cent either way. They may well be more numerous elsewhere. I should like to add here that, in working on family history, I owe a deep debt to several local historians and friends, particularly to Mr Norman Scarfe in Suffolk.

[1] E. C. Lodge, ed., *The Account Book of a Kentish Estate, 1616–1704*, 1927, *passim*; B.M., Add. MS 34162, *passim*; Loan 18, Capel Cure MSS, Henry Oxinden's Diary and Memorandum Book; Everitt, *Community of Kent*, pp. 29–33. Altogether Henry Oxinden spent £1,420 between 1629 and 1649 in improving the little manor-house of his grandfather. Modification of and addition to existing structures, rather than a complete rebuilding, were also characteristic of English towns at this period, for example in places like King's Lynn.

Jacobean prodigy houses, like Wollaton, Burghley, Cobham, and Longleat, are not really representative of the way of life and the origins of the vast majority of the gentry in England. Far more characteristic, even of the greatest families, were the old patchwork houses like Scots' Hall and Penshurst in Kent, or Delapré and Nevill Holt in the Midlands: houses basically medieval in plan, but extended and adorned at various dates in the sixteenth and seventeenth centuries.[1] Almost always, at this date, such homes were farms as well as manor houses. Their life was still rooted in the soil in a way in which the 'gentlemen's seats' of Georgian England, behind their palings and shrubberies, were not. They were still the centres of a local agrarian commonwealth.

The sense of quiet continuity with the past in such houses is described by Sir Philip Sidney, in a passage in *Arcadia*, which so obviously applies to his own home at Penshurst as to bear quoting in full. "The house itself", he says, "was built of fair and strong stone, not affecting so much any extraordinary kind of fineness, as an honourable representing of a firm stateliness. The lights, doors and stairs, rather directed to the use of the guest, than to the eye of the artificer: and yet as the one chiefly heeded, so the other not neglected; each place handsome without curiosity, and homely without loathsomeness: not so dainty as not to be trod on, nor yet slubbered up with good fellowship; all more lasting than beautiful, but that the consideration of the exceeding lastingness made the eye believe it was exceeding beautiful."[2] If these remarks were true of Penshurst, they were at least equally true of the many village manor houses of England, too small for the architectural historian to comment upon, though quite as important to the historian of provincial life.

II THE ELEMENTS OF CONSERVATISM

THESE three general observations about English society have been made because they help to explain the strength and tenacity of that provincial world which, in the last resort, defeated both Charles I in the thirties and Cromwell in the fifties. For, as already remarked, any theory of social development in this period must endeavour to explain the Restoration as well as the Civil War. But what were the social and economic forces behind this strength and tenacity? Once again only a handful of the more important topics can be mentioned.

[1] Scots' Hall no longer exists; but eighteenth- and nineteenth-century engravings and descriptions of it show it to have been of this type.

[2] Sir Philip Sidney, *The Countess of Pembrokes Arcadia*, ed. A. Feuillerat, 1922, p. 15. According to Clarendon 'good fellowship'—in other words drunkenness—was a vice generally spread over the county of Kent (*History of the Rebellion*, ed. Macray, IV, p. 334).

The Distribution of Wealth

One of the principal factors was simply that the vast bulk of the nation's wealth in the seventeenth century was still in the hands of provincial people. The point is obvious, but it needs stressing. It can be illustrated from the figures for the Monthly Assessments levied by the central government on all the counties and cities of England between 1648 and 1660.[1] Like other taxation records, the assessments are not infallible, but on the whole they tally with other lines of evidence. The total sum to be raised, varying from £20,000 to £120,000 a month, was first allotted proportionately between the shires by parliament, and then redistributed by each county committee on the inhabitants within its jurisdiction. The county proportions appear to have been worked out with some care, and they were revised from time to time in order to bring them more closely into line with the wealth of each district. One major reallocation occurred, in 1649, when the sums assessed on the five most heavily burdened counties (Norfolk, Suffolk, Essex, Kent, and Devon) were reduced from 37·8 per cent of the total to 25·2 per cent. The levies on several undertaxed Midland and northern counties (e.g., Northamptonshire and Yorkshire) were at the same time considerably increased. Though interesting in themselves, these re-assessments do not, however, affect the point at issue. The levies both before and after 1649 show that the vast bulk of the nation's taxable wealth was in provincial hands, and not in those of Londoners. Until 1649 the city actually paid less tax than Norfolk, Suffolk, Essex, or Kent.[2] Even if we include West-minster and the whole of Middlesex (still in fact largely rural) it only paid a little more than Norfolk—9 per cent compared with 8·3 per cent. After 1649 the Norfolk figure was reduced to 5·4 per cent; but though the metropolis was once again expanding, it still paid only a little over 9 per cent of the nation's taxes.[3]

[1] See Appendix, Table I. The earlier parliamentary assessments have not been utilized because they do not usually cover the whole country, and during the war the economy of many counties was disrupted. For the method of apportioning the assessment within the shire, and the remarkable efficiency of the tax, cf. Everitt, *Community of Kent*, pp. 157–9.

[2] In Kent and Essex part of the assessments was, of course, borne by London suburbs. But in 1640–60 the suburban area was still very small. The whole lathe of Sutton-at-Hone in Kent, which comprises the area between London, Gravesend, Tunbridge Wells, and Cowden on the Sussex border, paid only 9 per cent of the county's assessment. It is very doubtful if the London suburbs paid more than one-sixth of this 9 per cent. The two easternmost of the county's five lathes (Shepway and St Augustine), by contrast, paid nearly half the Monthly Assessment on Kent. Until the nineteenth century west Kent was in general poorer and more thinly populated than east Kent (Everitt, *Community of Kent*, p. 159).

[3] The extent of rural land in Middlesex can be gauged from the early large-scale maps of the county. The tax assessments cannot be explained away as an attempt to favour London at the expense of royalist shires. Three of the four most heavily taxed counties—Essex, Suffolk, and Norfolk—were certainly not predominantly royalist. Their assessments were, it is true, considerably reduced in 1649; but those of other predominantly parliamentarian counties, such as Northamptonshire, were

The evidence of the assessments of 1648–60 is, on the whole, corroborated by that of the Hearth Tax Assessments of 1662. Of the 1,618,535 recorded hearths in England, 156,361, or 9·7 per cent, were in London, Westminster, and Southwark.[1] If we suppose that one-third of the Middlesex total (excluding Westminster) of 94,508 hearths and all the hearths in the partially suburbanized parishes of Essex, Surrey, and Kent (19,285) were essentially metropolitan, the full figure for the whole conurbation was about 12·8 per cent of the total.[2] This is, of course, a very remarkable proportion, and more will be said later of the impact of metropolitan wealth in the provinces. But it must not blind us to the fact that the provincial figure was at least seven times as great as that of the whole metropolitan area—between 85 and 90 per cent of the total.

It may be argued that much of this provincial wealth was in the hands of peers and magnates whose life was largely centred on London and the Court, even though their estates were in the country. How far the life of such people was in fact oriented towards the capital and how far rooted in the shires is a point on which a good deal might be said.[3] In the counties which I have studied most of the peers and a few of the baronets frequented the metropolis fairly regularly for part of the year. The great majority of the knights and virtually all the squires, on the other hand, rarely if ever visited it, except to attend an occasional lawsuit (not a circumstance likely to endear it to them), and virtually never possessed a town house at this date. As is well known, there were many proclamations during the early seventeenth century banishing the gentry from London back to their native shires. But what these proclamations do not reveal is that in a large county, such as Suffolk or Kent, there might be 750–1,000 gentry, and that at least three-quarters of them were small parochial squires with an average income of less than £300 a year. Such families could

sharply increased. On the whole the evidence of the assessments gives a similar picture of the distribution of wealth, as between the counties, to that afforded by the history of inland trade and agriculture in this period.

[1] The percentages are calculated from the figures for each county given in C. A. F. Meekings, ed., *Dorset Hearth Tax Assessments, 1662–1664*, 1951, pp. 108–9. The county proportions are of considerable interest: see Appendix, Table II.

[2] For the Middlesex parishes full details do not survive for 1662 and the 1666 figures are not strictly comparable. The assumption that half the county total was properly metropolitan is therefore guesswork, but can hardly be incorrect, so far as the metropolitan total is concerned, by more than 1 per cent either way. The parishes reckoned as suburban in Essex, Kent, and Surrey are: West Ham, Deptford, Greenwich, Southwark Liberties in Surrey, Lambeth, Bermondsey, Rotherhithe, Newington, Battersea, Clapham. Considerable stretches of some of these parishes were still rural in 1662. The suburban figures for Surrey have been taken from the 1664 assessments, in the absence of figures for 1662.

[3] There is a good deal of evidence in Lawrence Stone, *Crisis of the Aristocracy, 1558–1641*, 1965. I have myself ventured some opinions on the subject in: 'The Peers and the Provinces', in *The Agricultural History Review*, xvi, i, 1968; and in 'The County Community', in *The English Revolution*, ed. Eric Ives, 1968.

obviously never have afforded a metropolitan establishment.[1] They were essentially provincials, though not necessarily by any means the boozy squires of Whiggish legend.

Even if we grant that the peers and leading provincial magnates were not in any true sense rooted in the countryside, we should still have to decide what their stake in the kingdom's wealth really was. If the situation in Yorkshire and Kent is any guide, their importance can be exaggerated. In Kent at least 90 per cent of the wealth of the community, and possibly more than 95 per cent, was in the hands of social classes wholly rooted in the shire: whereas only 5–10 per cent, at the most, was in the hands of peers and magnates. These proportions have been arrived at in the following way. The total landed income of all the armigerous families of Kent was probably in the region of £330,000 a year.[2] Of this total the 10 peers, 31 baronets, and 50 knights each received, as a group, about 12 or 13 per cent, and the 750 untitled squires 61 per cent. As far as it is possible to judge, this figure of £330,000 was probably not more than 35 or 40 per cent of the total taxable income of the shire. We know this because between 1643 and 1645 the county was paying £100,000–£116,000 per annum in assessments, and these were based on a poundage rate of 2s. 6d. The total income of Kent appears, then, to have been at least £800,000–£928,000 a year, or a mean figure of £864,000. There is some reason to suppose that it may in fact have been considerably greater, possibly even twice as much.[3] But if we take it to be no more than £864,000, the peers received only 4·7 per cent of the total and the baronets 5·1 per cent; whereas the knights and squires together received 28·5 per cent, and the non-armigerous families of all types 61·7 per cent. Taken as a whole, then, the families who were indubitably rooted in Kent—husbandmen, yeomen, tradesmen, craftsmen, and untitled squires, together with most of the knights and baronets and one or two indigenous Kentish peers like Lord Teynham—seem to have possessed at least nine-tenths of the taxable wealth of the county, and possibly more than 95 per cent. There is nothing surprising in the fact that the people of Kent fought for their local

[1] Everitt, 'The Peers and the Provinces', p. 61.

[2] See Appendix, Table III(b). For the method of calculating this income see 'The Peers and the Provinces', p. 61.

[3] Everitt, *Community of Kent*, p. 160. The poundage rate of 2s. 6d. suggests that taxation amounted to 12·5 per cent of income. In the one ascertainable case over a long period, that of Nicholas Toke of Godinton, it was only 5 per cent of income between 1645 and 1660. Though the burden of taxation declined after the war was over, Toke's proportion suggests that the total county income may have exceeded £1½ m. This single instance may, of course, be untypical, and I know of no similarly continuous series of accounts in Kent by which it can be checked. In Gregory King's estimates, the total national income is given as £43½ m. Judged by the Kentish proportion of the Hearth Tax (5 per cent of the total for England), King's figure would suggest an income for Kent of about £2,175,000 in 1688. (Cf. Andrew Browning, ed., *English Historical Documents*, VIII, 1660–1714, 1966, pp. 516–17.)

world in 1648 with a fierceness which astonished Westminster. The county had shown itself equally obstructive to Charles I in the 1630s, and was to do so yet again to Cromwell and to Charles II. Not unnaturally those who paid the piper sometimes felt they had a right to call the tune. And in the long run, despite many setbacks, they were not altogether unsuccessful in doing so.

In Yorkshire, despite certain significant differences in the social structure, the broad pattern of wealth seems to have closely resembled that in Kent. From figures for the gentry kindly supplied by Dr J. T. Cliffe, augmented for some of the peers from Professor Stone's calculations, a similar table to that for Kent has been compiled, showing the proportion of the county's income in the hands of peers, baronets, knights, and untitled families.[1] On this basis the total income of these groups was almost identical with that of their contemporaries in Kent: about £315,000 a year compared with £330,000. There were, it appears, fewer gentry as a whole in Yorkshire (691 : 841), and the average income of knights and baronets seems to have been somewhat higher: the legendary wealth of Kentish families was evidently exaggerated by contemporaries. The distribution of wealth as between knights and squires, moreover, was somewhat different in Yorkshire, since the former were exceptionally numerous and the latter less preponderant than in Kent (589 : 750).[2] But the proportion of wealth in the hands of these two groups together was almost identical: 72 per cent in Yorkshire as against 74 per cent in Kent. In both counties, moreover, the two topmost tiers in the social pyramid—peers and baronets—received together approximately one-quarter, or a little more, of the total income of the gentry.

What proportion do these Yorkshire figures bear to the total income of the county? No precise answer to this question is possible, because the taxation records of the period have not been worked over in detail, and may be less complete than in Kent. But there is reason to think that the county income may have been of the same order of magnitude as that of the latter shire at this time.

---

[1] See Appendix, Table III(a). I am deeply indebted to Dr Cliffe for his help. The research behind this paragraph is entirely his. It should be added that the income figures he has given me relate to gross income. They include all property descending in the main line, and no deduction has been made for annuities and rent charges to relations, lands charged with portions, mortgages, or extents. The Kentish figures were originally compiled in another connexion and where possible I subtracted such charges on the estate as annuities. To this extent the Kentish and Yorkshire figures are not comparable, and in some cases the disparity may be considerable. The proportion of wealth in magnates' hands in Yorkshire was, if anything, smaller than the figures in these paragraphs suggest.

[2] It should be said, however, that it is exceedingly difficult to compile an exhaustive list of the minor gentry of a county. The Kentish figure is only approximate. It includes many men reckoned armigerous by contemporaries, and whose standing is evidenced in church monuments and parish histories, but who never appeared before the Heralds at their visitations. It is impossible to be certain that none of these parochial gentry have been omitted. See also Appendix, Table III, footnote 3.

CHANGE IN THE PROVINCES

In the Monthly Assessments for 1648–60 Yorkshire paid 4·4 per cent of the total for England as against Kent's 5·2 per cent; but in the Hearth Tax Assessments of 1662 Yorkshire was rated at 6·9 per cent of the total (111,211 hearths) and Kent at 5 per cent (about 80,000).[1] It seems, therefore, that in the north as well as the south the families who were indubitably rooted in the area were probably possessed of at least nine-tenths of its total wealth, and possibly more than 95 per cent. Quite as much as Kent, it may be recalled, Yorkshire was (and still is) a county apt to make up its own mind in matters of politics. Evidently there was a solid economic basis for the traditional independence of its people.

The question remains whether the pattern of wealth in Yorkshire and Kent was typical of that in the rest of the kingdom.[2] In counties like Wiltshire and Lancashire, dominated as they were by magnates like the earls of Pembroke and Derby, the proportion of wealth in noble hands may well have been greater. It is doubtful, however, if it could ever have been overwhelming in any county. According to Professor Stone's calculations the total income of all the peers in England in 1641 was not more than about £800,000 a year, or probably a good deal less than the respective county incomes of Kent and Yorkshire. In fact the income of all the five richest peers in England together did not exceed £74,500 p.a., which was not much more than one-third of that of the untitled squirearchy in Kent alone.[3]

The figures utilized in the foregoing paragraphs, it must be remembered, are estimates. No one who seeks to work out family incomes in the seventeenth century can expect to arrive at more than tentative results. But they probably provide a reasonably reliable guide to the distribution of wealth in two counties, and the present writer would be surprised if the pattern was very different in such shires as Leicestershire, Northamptonshire, Norfolk, Suffolk, and Devon. Certainly the wealth of individual baronets, knights, and squires does not seem, on the whole, to have been very dissimilar.[4] It must be emphasized,

---

[1] Meekings, op. cit., pp. 108–9. See also Appendix, Table II.

[2] For what they are worth, the estimates of Thomas Wilson in 1601 and Gregory King in 1688 suggest that the proportion of wealth in the hands of the squirearchy, as compared with the peers, was a good deal higher in England generally than these Yorkshire and Kentish figures imply. In all probability, however, both writers underestimated the peers' wealth and exaggerated that of the typical squire and gentleman. Their estimates are given in an appendix to Stone, op. cit., p. 767. Gregory King's figures, it should be said, are given in varying forms. Some of the totals cited by Professor Stone are rather higher than those given in Browning, op. cit., p. 516. King's figures have been severely criticized, so far as the social distribution of landed property is concerned, by Mr J. P. Cooper in Econ. Hist. Rev., 2nd Ser., xx, No. 3, Dec. 1967, pp. 432–4.

[3] Stone, op. cit., pp. 481, 761, 762.

[4] Cf. M. F. Keeler, The Long Parliament, 1640–41, 1954, biographical section, passim; Everitt, Suffolk and the Great Rebellion, p. 16.

however, that much more spadework needs to be done on the social structure and the wealth of other county communities in England, especially in the north and west, before we can arrive at very positive conclusions. There may well have been more variety in provincial society in these respects than we realize.

Regional Cultures and Capitals

Another factor of great importance in the insularity of provincial communities in the seventeenth century was the development of regional farming. Such regionalism was not altogether new, of course, for the broad distinction between the pastoral Highland Zone and the arable Lowland Zone was implicit in the climate and geology of Britain. Nor was its only effect to foster localism, for it also led to an increase in trade between different parts of the country which, for the wayfaring traders involved, tended to break through the barriers of native isolation. Nevertheless, as the work of Dr Joan Thirsk and others has shown, regional specialization in farming was increasing in the sixteenth and seventeenth centuries and accentuating many local differences even within the Highland and Lowland Zones.[1] Coupled with the rise of population and the progress of enclosure, amongst other diverse factors, it changed the rural economy of many agrarian districts. It led to the emergence of special skills and crafts peculiar to each region, and magnified the latent differences in their social structure.

It was in the sixteenth century in Kent, for example, that extensive orchards were first established around Faversham and Sittingbourne; that hops began to be cultivated on a large scale near Canterbury and Maidstone; and that commercial barley-farming became characteristic of the Isle of Thanet. Each of these specialized types of husbandry led to certain peculiarities in local society. Each district developed characteristics of its own marking it off from the pastoral communities of the Weald and from the forest hamlets of the chartlands, that is, the wooded ragstone area between the downs and the Weald. In each the changing social pattern tended to produce acute problems of social disorder. The new farming methods necessitated a large migration of workfolk each summer, from the pastoral areas of the county, to gather in the fruit and hops and to reap the barley-fields. Crowds of farmworkers thronged the fields and lanes of east Kent and were temporarily housed by their employers in barns, shacks, booths, outhouses, and menservants' chambers in the farmhouses.[2] In Thanet the high wages and drunken demeanour of these migrants

---

[1] Cf. Joan Thirsk, ed., *The Agrarian History of England and Wales*, IV, 1500–1640, chapters I and VII.
[2] Cf. H.M.C., *Portland*, II, p. 280. Kentish probate inventories often refer to these 'menservants' chambers' or 'folks' chambers'.

so exacerbated the endemic lawlessness of the region that at one time a proposal was put forward to form the island into a separate county, with a sheriff and assizes of its own.

In the pastoral areas of the Weald of Kent other developments were at work in rural society, producing equally acute problems for the authorities, though of a different kind. The rapid increase in the Wealden population during the sixteenth century drove many families either to supplement their income from husbandry by taking up various kinds of by-employment, usually some form of woodcraft, or else to engage in the cloth and iron industries of the region. Such occupations tended to develop strong traditions and recondite skills of their own, and since they were often handed down in the same family from one generation to the next, they also strengthened the sense of local cohesion and the structure of family life. The region was in any case one where manorial control was weak, major gentry were few, and independent yeomen exceptionally numerous and powerful. Many of the parishes of the Weald, moreover, were unusually large—several of more than 10,000 acres—and most people lived in scattered hamlets or isolated farms at a distance from their parish church, often as much as four or five miles away. For such families there was obviously no possibility of getting to church more than once in a while, and the hamlets they inhabited either remained virtually heathen or became fruitful seedbeds for dissenting sects, sometimes of the weirdest description. As a consequence the Wealden area bred an intensely insular society, and one that was usually regarded by outsiders with some aversion. By one typical observer it was described as "that dark country which is the receptacle of all schism and rebellion." Characteristically it played no part in the Kentish uprising of 1648 in which the rest of the county was engaged, partly because of its puritanism, but perhaps chiefly because of its aloofness and isolation.[1]

In other regions of England rural society was no less insular in its forms and proclivities. Several of the forest areas elsewhere, there is reason to think, resembled the Weald in their peculiar mixture of heathen survival and rural dissent. The scattered nature of their settlement, the weakness of their manorial structure, the tenacity of their feuds and family life, the growth of squatters' communities within them, their relative remoteness from authority, and the lawlessness of certain sections of their population combined to encourage the propensity to independence and dissent. Like the Weald they often earned unfavourable comments from contemporary travellers, and they also aroused the distrust of more law-abiding communities in fielden parishes nearby.[2]

[1] Thirsk, op. cit., p. 112; Everitt, Community of Kent, passim.
[2] For some of the characteristics of these forest settlements, see my chapter on 'Farm Labourers' in Thirsk, op. cit., pp. 399, 404, 409–12, 462–4.

According to John Aubrey the inhabitants of woodlands were "mean people [who] live lawless, nobody to govern them, they care for nobody, having no dependence on anybody." According to John Norden "the people bred amongst woods are naturally more stubborn and uncivil than in the champion countries." They were, he said, "given to little or no kind of labour, living very hardly with oaten bread, sour whey, and goats' milk, dwelling far from any church or chapel, and are as ignorant of God or of any civil course of life as the very savages amongst the infidels". In Wiltshire, said Aubrey, the woodland area was "a sour, woodsere country, and inclines people to contemplation. So that the Bible, and ease, for it is all now upon dairy grassing and clothing, set there with a-running and reforming."[1] In the neighbourhood of Blean Forest in east Kent, John Wesley at a later date described the inhabitants as indeed "called Christians, but more savage in their behaviour than the wildest Indians" he had met with in America.[2]

These quotations, it is true, come from hostile observers. In all probability they were more strictly applicable to the newer squatters' communities of forest areas than to the socially more diversified indigenous settlements. Yet they can be corroborated by evidence from less partial sources. In Northamptonshire, for instance, it is not difficult to establish that the forests of Rockingham and Whittlewood were the principal areas of rural puritanism in the county, and that they were also prone to witchcraft survivals and to strange sectarian experiments.[3] Certainly it was primarily in areas of scattered and woodland settlement, like Kingswood and Wychwood Forests, and parts of Devon, Northamptonshire, Shropshire, East Anglia, and the West Riding, that the early Evangelical Revival under Philip Doddridge and John Wesley found many of its rural adherents in the following century.[4]

Among the gentry, it may be thought, this kind of regional insularity must have been less pronounced. In all probability it was so, but in 1640 it was still surprisingly powerful. In the counties I have worked on in lowland England,

[1] Quoted in Thirsk, op. cit., pp. 111, 112, 411.

[2] Quoted in Richard Green, John Wesley: Evangelist, 1905, p. 176. Wesley is said to have been preaching at or near Faversham, on the edge of Blean Forest. It is possible he was referring to the townsmen, but more probably to the forest inhabitants, who were notoriously lawless. The church of Dunkirk was built in the following century specifically to 'civilize' the area, following the insurrection of John Nichols Tom, alias Sir William Courtenay, who had founded a sect of his own in the forest, and eventually claimed to be the Messiah. The story of Tom's sect and its disastrous termination is told in P. G. Rogers, Battle in Bossenden Wood, the Strange Story of Sir William Courtenay, 1961.

[3] One such sect, near Brackley, maintained a continuous dance, round the clock, in expectation of the Second Advent.

[4] These last two sentences are based on research into the distribution of nonconformity in Northamptonshire, on the copious contemporary witchcraft literature for the county, and on an analysis of the subscribers' lists of the writings of Philip Doddridge, the Northampton Congregational leader. I hope to publish my findings on these topics in more detail in the near future.

farming was still the basis of wealth for most of the gentry. Very often they took a direct personal interest in it and farmed much of their own estates themselves. In Leicestershire, according to Defoe at the end of the century, "most of the gentlemen are graziers, and in some places the graziers are so rich that they grow gentlemen . . ." In Yorkshire, too, many of the gentry engaged in the commercial farming of their estates.[1] In Suffolk the property of most of the gentry must have been well under 1,000 acres in extent and they could not have afforded to cast over it the casual eye of a Georgian duke. In Kent, families like the Twysdens and Oxindens knew every field and hedgerow of their modest estates personally, as their tenants must have sometimes realized perhaps too acutely. Men like Nicholas Toke kept careful farm-account books, and several Kentish squires wrote treatises on various aspects of husbandry. One of the most influential of these discourses was Reginald Scott's well-known book, *A Perfect Platform of a Hop-Garden*. Another, probably intended for circulation in manuscript amongst neighbouring squires, was Sir Edward Dering's *Orchard, or a Book of Planting . . . with the Art and Husbandry belonging even from the Kernel*.[2] This volume was compiled in the 1630s and contains detailed notes on the culture and fruiting of about 150 varieties of trees in his orchards at Surrenden Dering, a few miles from Ashford. The fact that such books were written shows the widespread interest in farming amongst the local gentry.[3]

The self-centred character of the farming regions of England was in many ways intensified by the remarkable expansion of market towns between 1570 and 1640, and especially by the rise of the county capitals. Towns were the places where the inhabitants of the region met—to buy, to sell, and to talk. On market days a borough like Northampton focused the life of the county community around it. It was the mart for news and gossip as well as for trade.

---

[1] Everitt, *Community of Kent*, pp. 25 sqq; Daniel Defoe, *A Tour through England and Wales*, Everyman edn, 1959, II, p. 89; *ex inf*. Dr J. T. Cliffe.

[2] The manuscript was in the Phillipps Collection and came on the market in 1967. The details above are taken from Messrs Sotheby's *Catalogue of the Celebrated Collection of Manuscripts formed by Sir Thomas Phillipps, Bt. (1792–1872)*, N.S., Pt. III, 1967, p. 57.

[3] There is some evidence for a decline in this interest in the Restoration period, and for a growing tendency for the greater gentry to become mere *rentiers*. Nicholas Toke's grandson and heir, for example, failed to take close personal care of his property in Kent. The decline may have been fostered by the growth of estates due to their amalgamation through intermarriage, which led to the gradual decrease in numbers of the smaller gentry in counties like Kent and Devon. Possibly, however, it was only a temporary decline. It was partly due to the restless temperament of the Cavaliers who had been uprooted from their estates during the Civil War and Interregnum, and who seem to have found it hard to settle down again to the humdrum tasks of estate management. The same restlessness was evident in the rapid increase of travel amongst the gentry after the Restoration. For this latter phenomenon see E. A. L. Moir, *The Discovery of Britain: the English Tourists, 1540–1840*, 1963; W. G. Hoskins, *Provincial England: Essays in Social and Economic History*, 1963, chapter XI, 'The Rediscovery of England'.

Country people came into the town on all the nine or ten main roads, from Daventry, Brackley, Towcester, Bedford, Peterborough, Kettering, Leicester, Lutterworth, and Coventry. They left their horses at the inns or arrived on foot or by wagon. In the early eighteenth century there were about 60 inns in Northampton, and their stables were probably able to accommodate about 4,000 horses. Even in smaller centres, such as Bruton and Win-canton in Somerset and Redruth in Cornwall, several thousand people are said to have come into market each week in the seventeenth and eighteenth centuries.[1]

For the knights and squires of the region as well as for farmers and traders the county town provided a meeting place. As they increased in wealth and numbers under the Tudors and Stuarts, as their economic activities prolifer-ated and the burdens of local administration multiplied, their visits to the shire-towns also became more frequent, and further functions were added to the traditional activities of the old county capitals.[2] The first town houses of the country gentry began to appear in places like Bury St Edmunds and North-ampton about the end of Queen Elizabeth's reign.[3] About the same time some of the major urban inns, like the Star at Maidstone, the George at North-ampton, and the Three Cranes at Leicester, began to assume the functions of a county hall, where the gentry foregathered to discuss the news of the shire, resolve its administrative problems, and air its grievances.[4] In the remarkable rise of county self-consciousness in this period the emergence of the county town as the centre of the social, political, economic, and administrative life of the region was scarcely less important than the rise of the gentry themselves. The fact that such towns were small, rarely numbering more than 5,000 in-habitants, does not affect the issue. Their significance lay in their function as

[1] Everitt, 'Farm Labourers', in Thirsk, *op. cit.*, p. 451; *The Travels through England of Dr Richard Pococke*, Camden Society, N.S., XLII, 1888, p. 113. The inns of Salisbury in the 1680s could accom-modate nearly 900 horses (cf. N. J. Williams, ed., *Tradesmen in Early-Stuart Wiltshire*, Wilts. Arch. and Nat. Hist. Soc., Records Branch, XV, 1960, p. xv). If the situation in Northampton is any guide, per-haps as many again could be stabled in the yards and outbuildings of premises other than inns.

[2] Dr Hassell Smith gives an excellent description of the busy-ness of a county town at quarter-sessions or assize-time in 'Justices at work in Elizabethan Norfolk', *Norfolk Archaeology*, XXXIV, ii, 1967, p. 93.

[3] Some of the nobility had houses in towns like Exeter long before the Tudor era (cf. W. G. Hoskins, *Fieldwork in Local History*, 1967, p. 105). But the town house of the country gentleman, occupied for the season in the local county capital, is essentially a phenomenon of the period from Queen Elizabeth on-wards. In some areas it emerged even later. The Heselrige Mansion in Gold Street, Northampton, is a good example of one of these seventeenth-century town houses. In this town, unlike some others, most of the mansions of the gentry were in the suburbs, not in the centre of the borough.

[4] Some valuable studies of this development of county government in this period include: T. G. Barnes, *Somerset, 1625–1640: a County's Government during the "Personal Rule"*, 1961; W. B. Willcox, *Gloucestershire: a Study in Local Government, 1590–1640*, 1940; A. Hassell Smith, 'Justices at Work in Elizabethan Norfolk', *Norfolk Archaeology*, XXXIV, ii, 1967, pp. 93–110.

the *forum* of the county community. The story of their cultural development in the seventeenth century is beyond the scope of this paper, but it is an important and neglected chapter in the history of seventeenth-century England.[1]

Kinship and Cousinage

Another factor of importance in the tenacity of local loyalty and its sense of continuity with the past was the patriarchal element in provincial society. The sense of belonging to a great cousinage and of being dominated by its claims was in several ways increasing in the sixteenth and seventeenth centuries. In Suffolk, for example, it became a powerful factor in the county's relative unanimity in this difficult period. In the words of Robert Reyce, the gentry of Suffolk were in the habit of meeting often, "conversing most familiarly together, which so winneth the good will one of another with all reverent regard of the meaner sort, true love and unfeigned affection of their neighbours, that if differences do arise, which are very seldom, such is the great discretion ever tempered with love and kindness among them, that these divisions are soon smothered and appeased." Doubtless Reyce's view of his native county was idyllicized; but it was not altogether without foundation.[2]

The same paternal conditions, though not as a rule the same unity, obtained in other shires. In Kent such conditions played a major part in the revolt of the county in 1648. Through the meetings of the gentry in one another's manor houses at that time, the forces of discontent gradually fused together and were eventually able to overthrow the structure of local government.[3] Even in a divided county, like Leicestershire, family loyalty and local connexion drew many minor gentry together, in support of the dominant Hastings family of Ashby de la Zouch on one side, and of the Greys of Bradgate on the other. In these counties the forces of kinship and neighbourhood often cut across the nascent political loyalties of the age. Political motives were not absent, but in the social conditions of the seventeenth century they could operate only through a network of family connexion.

The rise of this kind of clan-loyalty within the county communities of the

---

[1] Defoe, in his *Tour*, gives many graphic pen-sketches of the county towns in his day: see, for example, his remarks on Derby, Maidstone, Nottingham, and Shrewsbury. See also P. Heylyn, *A Help to English History*, 1709 (first published 1641), for brief contemporary descriptions of county towns like Bury St Edmunds in the mid-seventeenth century. The best modern studies of such a place in print are Sir Francis Hill, *Tudor and Stuart Lincoln*, 1956, and *Georgian Lincoln*, 1966. Lincoln, however, does not seem to have shared the prosperity of its sister-capitals in the seventeenth century. It was off the main thoroughfares of England, and, to judge from the Hearth Tax and Monthly Assessments, the county was relatively poor in relation to its vast acreage.

[2] Robert Reyce, *Suffolk in the XVIIth Century: the Breviary of Suffolk by Robert Reyce, 1618*, ed. Lord Francis Hervey, 1902, p. 60; Everitt, *Suffolk and the Great Rebellion*, Introduction.

[3] Everitt, *Community of Kent*, chapter VII.

time is of great importance in the study of the Civil War. It arose gradually and naturally, as we have seen, from the increasing tendency of the gentry to marry within their own local ranks, instead of beneath them or beyond the shire. One of the consequences of this tendency was the preoccupation of the gentry with matters of genealogy and heraldry. At first sight this interest may seem to be merely the childish concern of the upstart to discover a grandfather. Snobbery in it there certainly was; but for the historian there is more in the phenomenon than this. Its significance lies in the fact that these country gentry were not interested simply in the history of their own family, but in that of their county community as a whole.

One of the earliest examples of this interest in the family history of the shire as a whole may be seen in Kent, at Canterbury Cathedral. When the cloister was rebuilt early in the fifteenth century the operation was largely financed by the leading local families and the nobility, and their arms were incorporated in a series of more than 800 carved bosses in the vaulting. This sense of family solidarity persisted remarkably long in Kent, and the compilation of county armorials remained a favourite pastime, there as elsewhere, for generations to come. It was one of the many hobbies of Sir Edward Dering, the Kentish leader in 1640 and knight of the shire in the Long Parliament. In 1626–7 Dering compiled a volume containing more than 1,200 coats of arms of his fellow-countrymen and kinsmen in Kent. If he had completed it (it covered only the letters A to F) it would probably have comprised nearly 4,000.[1]

By the end of the sixteenth century this same interest in county genealogy was flourishing in all parts of the kingdom. In Yorkshire Sir William Fairfax's Great Chamber at Gilling Castle (completed in 1585) was decorated with a frieze depicting more than 370 coats of arms. In Northamptonshire Sir Christopher Hatton constructed three pyramids in his hall at Holdenby, covered with the arms of the gentry of the county, together with those of the peers of England.[2] At Exeter, when the New Inn was rebuilt after the Restoration, the arms of several of the leading families of Devon were incorporated in the elaborate plasterwork of the Apollo Chamber, where the gatherings of the county gentry were held.[3]

[1] His manuscript eventually came into the Phillipps Collection and was sold in 1967. A description of it is given in Messrs Sotheby's *Catalogue of the Celebrated Collection of Manuscripts formed by Sir Thomas Phillipps, Bt. (1792–1872)*, N.S., Pt. III, 1967, p. 56. The interest in family history in Kent went back at least to the fourteenth century, when a history of the Northwoods of Northwood Chasteners was written, one of the earliest family histories in England. This manuscript was also offered for sale at Sotheby's in 1967 and is described in the same catalogue, p. 61. Part of the history was published in translation in *Archaeologia Cantiana*, II, 1859, pp. 9–28. Many monuments in Kentish parish churches provide elaborate family genealogies: for example the Roberts monument at Cranbrook.

[2] *Ex inf.* Dr J. T. Cliffe; Stone, *op. cit.*, p. 25.

[3] Robert Dymond, 'The Old Inns and Taverns of Exeter', Devonshire Association, *Transactions*, XII, 1880, pp. 402–4. The plasterwork is said to have dated from 1689.

The ties of kinship and the local loyalties they engendered were not peculiar to the gentry, of course. Though they have rarely been studied in much detail for other classes, there is evidence for their existence in towns and villages too. At Dover, for instance, it was said in 1632 that the jurats or aldermen "were all linked together in kindred, uncle and cousin", just as the gentry of the county were around them. At Ipswich successive generations of Daundys, Sparrows, and Bloyses were prominent in the government of the borough from the early sixteenth century till the end of the seventeenth. In Northampton families like the Maynards, Mackerneses, Scrivens, and Lyons dominated the town for upwards of a century, and many businesses remained in the same hands for three or four generations. At Petworth there was a succession of Libards as millers, Barnards as chandlers, Lucases as locksmiths, Bowyers as shoemakers, and Haslens as barber-surgeons. At Leicester three freemen out of four followed in their fathers' footsteps in the sixteenth century. In the industrial parishes of Staffordshire it was common for businesses to pass from father to son, or to son-in-law and cousin, sometimes in unbroken descent until the eve of the Industrial Revolution. In the small towns of southern England, like Westerham and West Malling, trading establishments sometimes descended from father to son for three or four generations in succession. At Westerham several of the tradesmen who had acquired a new market for the town in James I's reign remained to influence its development until the end of the eighteenth century, gradually rising in the social scale to become wealthy innkeepers, local lawyers, and in one case a minor squire.[1]

There is urgent need for local investigations of these neglected trading dynasties of English towns. Many provincial churches contain memorials to half a dozen families of the kind, and there is plenty of other evidence in wills, inventories, freemen's lists, lawsuits, apprenticeship registers, and other records. They rarely developed into the rigid burghal hierarchies of continental cities, and in numbers they did not comprise more than a fraction of the urban population. But they were important beyond their mere numbers, since they formed an element of permanence and continuity in the web of urban life, and often played a prominent part in local government. In Northampton they were the people for whom the corporation drew up an elaborate code of precedence, governing their place in civic processions and

---

[1] Madeline Jones, *The Political History of the Parliamentary Boroughs of Kent, 1642–62*, London Ph.D. thesis, 1967, p. 42; Nathaniel Bacon, *Annalls of Ipswich*, 1884, *passim*; Northants. Record Office, Northampton wills and probate inventories; G. H. Kenyon, 'Petworth Town and Trades, 1610–1760: Part I', *Sussex Arch. Colls.*, xcvi, 1958, pp. 64–6; W. G. Hoskins, *Provincial England*, 1963, p. 110; for information on Staffordshire I am much indebted to Miss Marie Rowlands's unpublished study, 'The Probate Records of Staffordshire Tradesmen, 1660–1710'; Everitt, 'The Marketing of Agricultural Produce', in Thirsk, *op. cit.*, p. 477.

the way they should sit in the town church of All Saints.[1] When one enters All Saints today, rebuilt as it was in accordance with their own wishes after the fire of 1675, and sees their aldermanic pews, headed by the great mayoral throne, carved and gilded on its dais, one senses something of their patriarchal power in the urban community. It is a mistake to suppose that authoritarian forms of society in the seventeenth century were peculiar to the world of the country gentry. They were all but equally prominent in the old corporations too.

The course of inland trade in England in this period was itself shaped by similar channels of family influence and local connexion. There was little that was strictly impersonal about the inland commerce of Tudor and Stuart England. The supplies of cattle received by one London butcher, for instance, were arranged in conjunction with his own father and were often dispatched from the parental pastures in Lincolnshire. The Suffolk cheese-factor appointed by two London fishmongers was their own brother-in-law, Thomas Hoorth of South Elmham. A group of Thanet barley-farmers who sent malt to the capital in James I's reign were not only themselves related, but operated through London factors who were their own nephews and cousins. The purchase of fruit in Kent by London fruiterers, and their ownership of orchards in the countryside about Teynham, often arose from their intermarriage with the daughters of Kentish farmers and from the fact that they were themselves sons or cousins of Kentish yeomen. When the tenants of Sir Thomas Barrington in Essex wished to dispose of their surplus wool, Sir Thomas's steward wrote to his brother-in-law in London and his friend Mr Adames, either "to deal with some chapmen to come down hither out of Kent or some other places, [or] at least to give me speedy notice what rate wool yields with you, that so I may give intimation to some friends that perhaps will adventure to come themselves". In this way business enterprise in the provinces tended to operate through a network of kinship and personal connexion. Sons, fathers, brothers, cousins, wives, uncles, mothers, brothers-in-law: all were drawn into the circle.[2] Though the sense of belonging to a community, of being enthralled by its *esprit de corps*, was probably not as strong among these wayfaring merchants of

[1] The problem of seating local families in order of precedence in church was often a tricky one, especially in towns like Leicester, where it was changed from time to time by the churchwardens in accordance with a family's rise or decline in worldly substance. In 1575 Leicester corporation was involved in a lawsuit with the wrathful Mistress Joan Manby, who had been demoted from her accustomed seat, as wife of a former mayor, behind the reigning mayor's wife (cf. W. G. Hoskins, *Provincial England*, 1963, p. 110).

[2] Everitt, 'The Marketing of Agricultural Produce', in Thirsk, *op. cit.*, pp. 513, 557–8; cf. also pp. 523, 530–1. In Staffordshire Miss Rowlands has found (*op. cit.*) that the system of credit and capital-accumulation necessary to build up industrial concerns in the 1660–1710 period was almost always based on ties of marriage, neighbourhood, or religion.

England as it was among the county families of Kent and the urban dynasties of Northampton, it was nevertheless powerful and it was certainly on the increase.

Insecurity and Authority

Another important element in the social conservatism of the time was the underlying sense of insecurity in local society, and the consequent emphasis on social status and degree.[1] The local community was far more subject to natural and civil catastrophe then than it is today, and there was less to cushion the incidence of distress. The way in which the Great Rebellion rent apart the fabric of local society is now well documented; but the Rebellion itself needs to be seen also as one of a series of catastrophes to which seventeenth-century society was prone. Plague, fire, family bankruptcy, and harvest failure: these were personal tragedies that perpetually haunted the lives of ordinary provincial people. Their impact upon the local community needs more thorough examination than it has yet received.

The experience of many towns in the seventeenth century might be cited to illustrate the point; but a single instance will suffice. In the year 1605, as a result of plague, one person in every six in Northampton died: the equivalent, size for size, of more than 20,000 people in the town of today, or one and a half millions in London. A generation later, in 1638, another sixth of the inhabitants perished in a second visitation of the same disease. Less than forty years later, in 1675, four-fifths of the town was destroyed by fire and nearly 1,000 families were rendered homeless. The wealth that many of the townspeople had spent half a lifetime in accumulating went up in flames in three hours.[2] As contemporary tracts reveal, the effect of these disasters on Northampton was overwhelming. The townsmen's resilience was remarkable; but their mental outlook, as well as the economy of the town, was profoundly influenced by their experiences in time of fire and plague. Such events helped to shape their re-

[1] For attitudes to degree and status in the sixteenth and seventeenth centuries see, inter alia, the following: Austin Woolrych, 'Puritanism, Politics, and Society' in The English Revolution, ed. Eric Ives, 1968; A. L. Rowse, The England of Elizabeth, 1964 edn, pp. 20, 532; David Ogg, England in the Reigns of James II and William III, 1957, chapter III; Charles Wilson, England's Apprenticeship, 1603–1763, 1965, chapter I; Everitt, 'Farm Labourers', in Thirsk, op. cit., p. 461. The theme is of course prominent in Shakespeare and Hooker, and in many minor authors like Sir Robert Filmer and Sir Edward Dering. Even within the ranks of labourers there was a distinct social hierarchy at this time.

[2] See Tobias Coldwell's contemporary History of Northampton (MS copy in Northampton Borough Library), n.p.; A True and Faithful Relation of the late Dreadful Fire at Northampton [1675]; C. H. Hartshorne, Historical Memorials of Northampton, 1848, pp. 231 sqq.; J. C. Cox, ed., The Records of the Borough of Northampton, II, 1898, p. 238. In 1605, 625 people died (compared with an average of 139 p.a. for five normal years), and in 1638, 665 (compared with an average of 122). The population of the town at this time was probably between 3,500 and 4,000, or perhaps a little more.

ligious consciousness, with its pessimism, its puritanism, and its will-power. There can be no doubt that their vulnerability to catastrophe also made them more willing to accept the authoritarian and patriarchal forms of contemporary society. The corporation of Northampton was not prone to welcome interference by the country gentry; but it is doubtful if, in 1675, it could have recovered at all without the vigorous measures of relief instituted by the lord lieutenant and the county justices.[1]

Most widespread of all the problems of social order in the seventeenth century were those arising from the failure of the harvest. In an agrarian country, where the largest cities as much as the smallest hamlets were dependent on home-grown food, the failure of the harvest was an event with disastrous consequences. Unlike plague and fire, moreover, corn-shortage was not an occasional event, occurring once or twice in a generation: it was frequent and persistent. According to Professor Hoskins, 35 harvests were seriously deficient out of 140 between 1480 and 1619, and between 1620 and 1759 no fewer than 37.[2] Abundant harvests occurred, on average, four times in every ten years throughout this period; but in some decades there was a long run of bad years and only one or two good ones. In the 1630s, for instance, there was not a single good harvest till the end of the decade, in 1639. In consequence it was a time of high prices and urgent government action in all spheres of social policy. There was certainly a connexion between these economic problems and the political malaise of the period.

The early 1640s, by contrast, were a time of relative abundance; but in 1646 another series of bad harvests ensued, continuing without a good year until the 1650s. In five years (1646–50) the general price-level of foodstuffs rose by nearly 50 per cent.[3] Once again there was a connexion between economic distress and political unrest. The rebellion at Canterbury at Christmastime, 1647, which sparked off the Kentish rising of 1648, was aggravated by the local scarcity, poverty, high prices, and acute unemployment following the failure of the harvest.[4] Finally, in 1657, after a run of abundant years during the Protectorate, a third period of deficiency commenced, culminating in the dearth

---

[1] Northampton's experience of misfortune was not untypical, and perhaps less catastrophic than that of some larger towns. Mr J. F. Pound tells me that the population of Norwich seems to have fluctuated between 13,000 and 32,000 at different dates in the seventeenth century.

[2] This paragraph is principally based on W. G. Hoskins's two articles on 'Harvest Fluctuations' in *The Agricultural History Review*, XII, i, 1964 (covering the period 1480–1619) and XVI, i, 1968 (covering 1620–1759). See also Everitt, 'The Marketing of Agricultural Produce', in Thirsk, *op. cit.*, pp. 575–7. Professor Hoskins defines a harvest as 'deficient' if the average price was 10 per cent or more above the norm, and as 'abundant' if it was 10 per cent or more below (based on a 31-year moving average).

[3] According to the Phelps-Brown index of food prices cited by Professor Hoskins (base period 1451–75 = 100) the figures were: 1646, 569; 1647, 667; 1648, 770; 1649, 821; 1650, 839.

[4] Madeline Jones, *op. cit.*, p. 439.

of 1661–2, when prices rose to greater heights than in 1650. Those who lived through the Civil War and Commonwealth period suffered no fewer than ten harvest failures within fifteen or sixteen years. In the conditions of the seventeenth century these fluctuations were especially serious because the English economy worked on a fine margin between sufficiency and shortage. Probably quite one-third of the population lived so close to the poverty line that even a modest rise in prices, of 10 per cent or so, meant semi-starvation for them.

The problem was accentuated by certain changes in the methods of marketing which occurred between 1570 and 1640, and by the conflicting claims of various sections of the community, in particular upon the barley harvest.[1] Barley was usually the crux of the problem at this time because it was both the usual bread-corn of the poor and the principal raw material of the rapidly expanding brewing industry. The rise of the malting and brewing industry in the period 1570–1640 was thus a crucial development in the English economy. In many towns it placed brewers and maltsters in a novel position, not only as the chief capitalists, but as the money-lenders of the local community. With their growth in power they were enabled to purchase the barley crop in advance of harvest, and to compel farmers to enter into bipartite bonds, usually with a penalty of double the contract price on yeomen who failed to deliver the goods. Farmers were prepared to agree to these rigorous terms because the arrangement gave them a guaranteed market; but if the harvest turned out deficient, they were compelled to meet the claims of the brewers and maltsters first, and the labouring classes went hungry.

Unless the government intervened, a drop of 10 per cent in the yield of the barley harvest was therefore likely to mean a reduction of possibly 30 or 40 per cent in the supply of bread-corn to the poor. As a rule the government reacted vigorously to these circumstances and directed local justices of the peace to release corn supplies by suppressing the brewers, maltsters, and alehouse-keepers.[2] Though this did not endear the Stuarts to these influential sections of the business community, it encouraged the poor to turn to the magistrate for protection, and it rendered them more willing to acquiesce in his authority. Not all local justices, needless to say, acted in these circumstances from motives of pure altruism; but in time of calamity their authority was a necessity to the poor, and the more conscientious amongst them came to be looked up to as father-figures in the local community. Certainly this was true of men like Sir Thomas Scott, Sir George Sondes, and Sir Roger Twysden in Kent.[3] It was also true of

[1] This paragraph is based principally on Everitt, 'The Marketing of Agricultural Produce', *op. cit.*, especially pp. 575–86.

[2] *Ibid.*

[3] For Scott cf. Everitt, 'Farm Labourers', *op. cit.*, p. 461. Cf. also the ballad upon him, written after

Sir Nathaniel Barnardiston in Suffolk. Sometimes obstinate and a little intimidating a man like Sir Nathaniel may have been, but it is clear that when he died he had come to be revered by the poor, and respected as "one of the top-branches amongst our Suffolk cedars."[1] An authoritarian form of society, such as men of this kind represented, was probably a necessity in seventeenth-century conditions if society itself was to survive.[2]

The vulnerability of the local community to calamity seems to have been on the increase in the sixteenth and seventeenth centuries. It increased with the growth of population and the growing pressure on corn supplies. True, the increase in harvest yields between 1500 and 1650 may have just kept pace with the growth of population.[3] But against this must be set the expanding commercial demands of brewers and maltsters, and the increase of the more vulnerable sections of society. The urgency of government action and the growing anxiety of justices' reports also suggest that the sense of insecurity was becoming more intense. It is difficult not to see a connexion between this increasing insecurity and the growing pessimism and religious sensibility of the period. No doubt insecurity was only one reason for this sensibility; yet it goes some way to explain the sense of sadness and death in so much contemporary thought and poetry.

Many of the Elizabethan and Jacobean poets express this preoccupation

his death, probably by his kinsman Reginald Scott, and quoted in W. Jerrold, *Highways and Byways in Kent*, 1914 edn, pp. 254–5:

> "His men and tenants wailed the day,
>   His kin and country cried,
> Both young and old in Kent may say,
>   Woe work the day he died. . .
>
> His house was rightly termed Hall,
>   Whose bread and beef was ready;
> It was a very hospital
>   And refuge for the needy. . .
>
> In justice he did much excel,
>   In law he never wrangled:
> He loved religion wondrous well,
>   But he was not new-fangled."

Scott's family continued this tradition and his widow was praised as "a great housekeeper".

[1] Samuel Fairclough, *The Saints' Worthiness . . .*, 1653, p. 12.

[2] A good example of the disastrous effects of weak manorial control on a Lancashire estate (Penwortham), belonging to King's College, Cambridge, is given in Joan Thirsk, 'The Farming Regions of England', *The Agrarian History of England*, IV, 1500–1640, 1967, p. 88.

[3] W. G. Hoskins, 'Harvest Fluctuations and English Economic History, 1620–1759', *The Agricultural History Review*, XVI, i, 1968, p. 27. The problem was complicated by the fact that population increased rapidly in some areas and in others remained relatively static. As pointed out below, the expanding areas were compelled to import corn from others, and this rendered them more vulnerable to harvest failure.

with the brevity of human life and the fragility of earthly society. It is found in Shakespeare's sonnets, for example:

"Since brass, nor stone, nor earth, nor boundless sea,
But sad mortality o'ersways their power,
How with this rage shall beauty hold a plea,
Whose action is no stronger than a flower?"

It occurs again in Sir Philip Sidney:

"O take fast hold! Let that light be thy guide
In this small course which birth draws out to death,
And think how evil becometh him to slide
Who seeketh heaven, and comes of heavenly breath."

One finds it also in the poems of Sir John Davies:

"I know my life's a pain and but a span;
I know my sense is mock'd in everything;
And, to conclude, I know myself a man—
Which is a proud and yet a wretched thing."

And once more it occurs in the wistful, haunting lines of Thomas Campion:

"Never weather-beaten sail more willing bent to shore,
Never tired pilgrim's limbs affected slumber more,
Than my wearied sprite now longs to fly out of my troubled breast:
O come quickly, sweetest Lord, and take my soul to rest!"

These quotations, it may be said, are from the poets of the time and may not represent the general tenor of contemporary thought. But the same half-longing, half-obstinate looking back to the past, was found amongst ordinary people too. Sometimes, as with Sir Edward Dering in Kent, it took the form of a search for the 'golden age' of the church, an effort to revive the 'primitive simplicity' of Christianity. Sometimes, as with Dering's more matter-of-fact cousin, Sir Roger Twysden, it led to a lifetime's search for legal precedent, in order to re-establish the true old English constitution, as he saw it, in a confused and changing world. "What is the opinion of these days", said Twysden, characteristically, about the year 1640, "I conceive not greatly material for such as seek the basis or foundation on which this Commonwealth is built, but how *former times, before the dispute came*, did interpret it". The same questing interest in the past explains also the remarkable efflorescence of historical studies at this time, especially the interest in local history between 1570 and 1640. No one expressed the motives behind this new concern with history in more telling terms than Robert Reyce, the Suffolk antiquary of James I's reign. "What can be more pleasing to the judicious understanding", said he, "than plainly to see before him the lively usage of elder times, the alteration of names clean worn out, the revolution of families now wholly extinguished, the traces of antiquity, the memorials of our honourable ancestors?"[1]

Happy is the people, said Carlyle, whose annals are blank in the history books. By the same token, perhaps, a nation preoccupied with its own past, like early seventeenth-century England, is surely an unhappy and insecure one. Yet in the last resort the feeling of change and decay in a sense also helped to deepen the channels of social conservatism in England at this time. The victims of insecurity, unless they are exceptionally talented or dramatic individuals, rarely become authors of radical change. What they have won they have won hardly, and they are loath to lose it. Those who have lost their family or their business, or experienced other personal sorrows, know too much of the tragic aspects of human existence to become doctrinaire revolutionaries.

III THE ELEMENTS OF CHANGE

THERE was much in the historical development of English society in the seventeenth century, then, that tended to enhance the diversity and insularity of provincial life, to deepen its conservatism, and accentuate its sense of continuity with the past. The proportion of wealth in provincial hands, the number of local gentry and yeomen, the development of regional farming, the remoteness of forest communities, the development of local government, the rise of the county towns, the patriarchal forms of society, the dynastic loyalties of armigerous and urban families, the growing interest in history and genealogy, the preoccupation with authority and degree, the problems of dearth and plague, the obstinacy of society's response to such problems: all these, and other developments, had by 1640 brought about a remarkably varied and vigorous life in the provinces, and yet at the same time had rather deepened the sense of continuity than dispelled it. Obviously, however, this is not a complete picture of the social developments of the time. There were transforming forces at work as well, and it is now time to turn to some of these elements of change. Frequently the new developments ran counter to the native forces of localism and diversity; but at times they rather modified or co-operated with them.

---

[1] Sir Roger Twysden, *Certain Considerations upon the Government of England*, Camden Soc., XLV, 1849, ed. J. M. Kemble, p. 128 (italics mine); Reyce, *op. cit.*, p. 2.

Dependent Communities

In the first place, although the vulnerability of society to natural catastrophe in many ways strengthened its conservatism, as we have seen, in other ways it tended to encourage change and experimentation. For it seems to have been in regions and communities where population was expanding most rapidly, and where in consequence the sense of insecurity was apt to be strongest, that puritanism and nonconformity tended to flourish. The sense of insecurity was itself more intense in some parts of England than others partly because the growth of population—from perhaps 2,600,000 in the country as a whole in the 1520s to 5,500,000 in 1688—was greater in some regions than in others.[1] For a variety of reasons it seems to have been greatest in some of the towns and in many of the woodland areas, such as the Weald of Kent, Rockingham Forest, the Forest of Dean, and the borders of Essex and Suffolk.[2] Unfortunately for their inhabitants, these wooded regions were areas with a predominantly pastoral economy, growing relatively little corn of their own. Like London and the provincial towns, therefore, they were compelled to import grain from the arable areas of the country.

Gradually, in fact, England was becoming more sharply divided in the sixteenth and seventeenth centuries between the relatively self-sufficient corn-producing districts on one hand, and what one might call these 'dependent communities'—the forest and pastoral areas, the provincial towns, and London—on the other. Because these latter communities were dependent, they were the first to suffer in time of dearth, and the sense of insecurity amongst them was apt to become peculiarly powerful. Although this was of course only one element in their historical development, there is reason to think that it intensified their propensity to religious enthusiasm. The subject is one on which more research needs to be done before we can arrive at very positive conclusions. But certainly the sense of insecurity seems to have intensified religious feeling and encouraged dissent in districts like Rockingham Forest and the Weald of Kent, and in towns like Northampton and Sandwich.[3] For insecurity, whether personal or social, has often been the seedbed of spiritual experiment, though not necessarily of social change.

---

[1] These are the estimates given in W. G. Hoskins, *loc. cit.* The 1688 figure is taken from Gregory King.

[2] For some references to this topic, cf. Everitt, 'Farm Labourers', *op. cit.*, pp. 409–11, and Joan Thirsk, 'The Farming Regions of England', *ibid.*, pp. 10–11.

[3] This seems clear from the local history of dissenting chapels in these two counties, and from the copious tract literature of the period 1640–1700. There was a marked connexion between Northampton's disasters in the fire of 1675 and the revival of religion in the town, which culminated under Philip Doddridge and the Evangelical Awakening.

The New Gentry

To turn next to a more familiar element of change in Stuart society, the new gentry. In this connexion it is only necessary to repeat a point made elsewhere: that there were great differences in the proportion of new families in different counties.[1] Their numbers were only to a limited extent due, as we might suppose, to the proximity of London. Sometimes this proximity was important: it may have been a decisive factor in Hertfordshire, for example.[2] But more significant, as a rule, was the structure of the rural economy in the area concerned, the pattern of local landownership, the resistance of the original society to intrusion, and the availability of large stretches of land for purchase. These were some of the reasons why there were few new families in 1640 in Kent, whereas there were many in Northamptonshire. In the former county, where the native community was deeply rooted, highly inbred, and remarkably cohesive, where manors and estates were small and seem to have come on to the market in scattered parcels, only one-eighth of the gentry were newcomers since Queen Elizabeth's reign. In the eastern half of the county, the proportion of new gentry was no more than 3 per cent, and in the Weald it was virtually nil.

In Northamptonshire, by contrast, at least one-third of the county had been royal forest, from which extensive grants were made to outsiders in the sixteenth and seventeenth centuries. The well-known estate of Farming Woods, for example, a few miles from Oundle, remained crown property till 1628, when it was granted by Charles I to Lord Mordaunt. In 1650 Mordaunt's son, the Earl of Peterborough, parted with the property to Sir John Robinson, a London merchant who in the following year became lord mayor. In 1652 Robinson also acquired another forest manor, Grafton Underwood. The local dynasty that he founded remained a well-known one in Northamptonshire, seated at the neighbouring Cranford Park, till the twentieth century. Of many other grants of forest land in Northamptonshire, a few may be cited. Brigstock Parks were granted by the crown to the Cecils in 1602; Geddington Woods to Lord Montagu in 1628; Earls Wood and Fotheringhay Parks to the heirs of the Earl of Devon in 1603; Cottingham Woods to Sir Christopher Hatton in 1572; Pipewell Woods and various stretches of coppice to the Hatton family in 1629; Rockingham Park to Sir Lewis Watson in 1638; Hanslope Park to Isaac Pennington in 1628; Paulerspury Park to the Throgmortons in 1551 and 1596; and Stoke Bruerne Park to Sir Francis Crane in 1629.[3] A further factor in the influx

---

[1] Alan Everitt, 'Social Mobility in Early Modern England', *Past and Present*, No. 33, April 1966, pp. 59–65. The following paragraph is principally based on this article and the sources cited therein.

[2] *Ex. inf.* Mr Lionel Munby.

[3] P. A. J. Pettit, *The Royal Forests of Northamptonshire: a Study in their Economy, 1558–1714* (Northamptonshire Record Soc.), 1968, pp. 189–93.

of new families to Northamptonshire was, no doubt, the extent of the enclosure movement in the county. To judge from the Findings of the Enclosure Commissioners (though these are admittedly not very reliable evidence where acreages are concerned), enclosure seems to have been even more widespread in this county than in the adjoining Midland shires.[1]

As a consequence Northamptonshire offered greater possibilities to the newly-rich to build up relatively large and compact estates than a county like Kent, where there was no enclosure at this time and virtually no royal forest. Not only do we find an unparalleled series of great palaces being built there under Elizabeth and James I, but a remarkable influx of complete outsiders to the shire. In 1640 as many as one-third of the 274 gentle families in Northamptonshire whose origins are readily traceable had settled there since 1603, and nearly three-quarters since 1500. In both counties there was certainly a connexion between these social developments and local politics. While Northamptonshire, with its many new families, was on the whole energetic, puritanical, and decisive, Kent, with its deeply-rooted local society, was obstructive, conservative, and Anglican—though very definitely not Laudian. We must be wary, of course, of building any determinist theory on these facts; many other causes, including personal ones, were also at work.

The Wayfaring Community

Another well-known transforming element was the commercial penetration of provincial society by London. Between Henry VII's reign and Charles I's the population of the metropolis quadrupled, and the demands of its food market rocketed. This has long been a familiar fact through the work of Professor Fisher, Professor Gras, and others, and needs no recapitulation here. But some modifications of the popularly accepted view seem perhaps necessary. There can be no doubt that London's commercial penetration was locally intense. But its influence was in fact restricted to islands or pockets of countryside, surrounded by whole tracts of land where traditional practices remained largely unaffected by metropolitan demands.[2] Penetration was usually most intense in

---

[1] The figures are cited by Dr Joan Thirsk in 'Enclosing and Engrossing', *The Agrarian History of England*, IV, 1500–1640, 1967, pp. 241, 242. In the 1517–19 Findings the Northamptonshire figure was 14,081½ acres (cp. Oxfordshire, 11,831 acres); in 1607, 27,335½ acres (cp. Lincolnshire, 13,420 acres). The Northamptonshire total of 41,417 acres was more than twice as high as in any other county cited by Dr Thirsk. The returns are too incomplete to bear much weight, but as is well known there was little or no enclosure in Kent during this period. In Huntingdonshire fairly extensive enclosure may have been due to investment by London businessmen (*ibid.*, p. 243).

[2] For a general discussion of this subject see Everitt, 'The Marketing of Agricultural Produce', *op. cit.*, pp. 513–16.

those areas accessible by water transport, such as the Faversham and Thanet areas of Kent, the parishes bordering the Suffolk estuaries, the middle Thames valley, or the Ouse basin as far upstream as Bedford. The limitation of transport was not so important in the case of livestock, which were sent to market on their own feet; but it was usually decisive in marketing grain, fruit, malt, hops, and other bulky commodities. Until the days of turnpikes, after 1660 or 1700, such goods as these were rarely carried great distances overland. As a consequence, only two or three miles south of the intensively farmed corn-growing areas of north Kent lay more extensive tracts of countryside, on the downs and in the Weald, which were still largely given over to peasant farming. The produce of these areas was probably not as a rule destined for London, but primarily for the needs of the locality and its little market towns, places like Tenterden, Ashford, and Wye. There was, after all, nothing surprising in this fact. Vast though London was by 1640, it was no larger than modern Coventry, and less than half the size of modern Dublin. It did not require more than a fraction of the farming production of the provinces, whose inhabitants were still fifteen or twenty times as numerous as those of the metropolis. The appetites of even a quarter of a million cockneys are not insatiable.

Partly as a result of metropolitan expansion, but still more because of the much larger growth in the provincial population, there was a great development in inland trade in England between 1570 and 1640. And there can be no doubt that this was one of the most potent forces of economic and social change in this period. The open market places of provincial towns gradually proved incapable, during this time, of accommodating the expanding demand. By 1640 much of the new trade was transacted outside the official 'open market', and was unregulated by local officers and borough corporations. It took place instead in the warehouses and above all in the inns of provincial towns. To meet it, a virtually new class of wayfaring traders came into being, ranging from small carriers and local corn-badgers to wealthy horse-dealers and barley-factors. Sometimes these men travelled over a dozen different counties, and indeed from Scotland in the north to London and Bristol in the south. Of course this development was not an entirely novel phenomenon. Itinerant wool-merchants were a common feature of the countryside long before Queen Elizabeth's reign. But there can be no doubt that this society of wayfaring traders expanded immensely in the later sixteenth and seventeenth centuries. The rapid growth in the number and size of commercial inns in towns like St Albans, Northampton, and York, sometimes a three- or four-fold increase in this period, is one of many proofs of it. By the year 1660 there were more than 30 inns in St Albans, and in Northampton probably at least 40.[1]

[1] Everitt, 'The Marketing of Agricultural Produce', *op. cit.*, pp. 559–62, 588–9. Most of the literature

The remarkable development of the carrying trade in the seventeenth century is another indication of the expansion in internal commerce. John Taylor's *Carrier's Cosmography*, published in 1637, shows that by that date there was a regular carrying service between London and all parts of the kingdom.[1] By the latter half of the seventeenth century, and probably by Charles I's reign, this carrying trade was affecting the economy even of the remoter counties, such as Staffordshire.[2] At Uttoxeter, for instance, the great cheese market of the north Midlands, metropolitan cheesemongers had set up a factor and agent, who purchased and dispatched cheeses to the value of £500 weekly by means of the local carriers. At Newcastle-under-Lyme, too, a similar cheese factorage had been established, and a weekly carrying service to London was in operation. At Walsall there were regular services to the metropolis and some of the town's metal-workers were selling their wares in the city. Not all the Staffordshire carriers travelled towards the south-east, of course; there were also many cross-country routes. The moorlands in the north of the county and the roads into Leicestershire were frequently traversed by wagons and pack-horses carrying salt out of Cheshire and returning laden with malt for the north-country brewers.

Most of these Staffordshire carriers, like their contemporaries elsewhere, were local men of quite modest substance. The teams of horses listed in their probate inventories indicate the small scale on which they operated. George Fenton, a carrier in the village of Yoxall, had a team of only four horses. Ralph Foster of Burslem had a team of five; John Taylor, also of Burslem, of six; Matthew Bakewell of Uttoxeter, of seven; Robert Urram of Walsall, of eight; Richard Beech of Talke, of nine; and William Fenton of Penkhull, of ten. Jonathan Eardesley of Lichfield seems to have been unusually rich amongst the Staffordshire carriers of his time, and at his death had as many as 16 mares in his stables. Probably he hired some of these out for riding, and certainly he was a man living in considerable style. He owned a well-furnished house of three storeys, with a warehouse attached, and left more than £500 worth of personal property behind him at his death. Eardesley was an exception; but the relatively small scale of operations of most of these Staffordshire carriers

---

on the history of inns is too popular and gossipy to shed much light on their use as markets. There are some interesting references, however, in Robert Dymond, 'The Old Inns and Taverns of Exeter', Devonshire Association, *Transactions*, XII, 1880, pp. 387 sqq. Otherwise the chief sources of information are lawsuits in the Courts of Requests and Chancery, and, later, advertisements in provincial newspapers.

[1] Cf. Virginia A. LaMar, *Travel and Roads in England* (Folger Booklets on Tudor and Stuart Civilization), 1960, pp. 18–19; H. J. Dyos and D. H. Aldcroft, *British Transport*, 1969, pp. 34–5.

[2] For the following account of Staffordshire carriers I am much indebted to Miss Marie Rowlands's unpublished paper, 'The Probate Records of Staffordshire Tradesmen, 1660–1710'.

should not blind us to the extent of trade in their hands. Only occasionally do we get a glimpse of the extent of the carrying trade in any document before Defoe's day; but when one learns that in 1643 the wagons of a train of carriers, arrested by the earl of Northampton near Daventry and laden with cheeses and other goods from Cheshire, were hauled by 57 horses, one realizes something of the volume of traffic on some of the main roads of England by the time of the Civil War.[1]

Meeting one another in the same towns, even in the same inns, year after year, the carriers, factors, and wayfaring merchants of England gradually became an increasingly distinct and self-conscious community during the seventeenth century. As we have seen, they often developed amongst themselves a strong sense of cohesion and *esprit de corps*. Largely as a consequence of their activities a number of major towns, such as Derby, Shrewsbury, Exeter, Doncaster, Northampton, and Salisbury, became either general emporia for a wide stretch of countryside, or inland entrepôts noted for the marketing of some particular commodity. By 1640, for instance, Northampton was already becoming, as Defoe later described it, "the centre of all the horse-markets and horse-fairs in England". Dealers, farmers, coachmen, wagoners, carriers, peers, and gentry, as well as factors for the parliamentarian armies in the Civil War, travelled from north and south, east and west, to attend its great horse-fairs. In such towns the larger inns sometimes had 30 or 40 rooms, and could accommodate more than 50 travellers, with two or three times that number of horses. A census of accommodation in the hostelries of England in 1686 shows that in the inns of Salisbury alone there were 548 beds and stables for 865 horses. Inns like these, as well as being hostelries, were markets, warehouses, hotels, information centres, posting-houses, and occasionally rudimentary banks.[2] Not surprisingly the provincial innkeeper was often an important figure in his own town. By 1640, in an inland entrepôt like Northampton, he was usually among the wealthiest members of the community. Not infrequently he became the local mayor.

In the age before newspapers, the influence of the community of wayfaring traders in spreading news and encouraging religious and political discussion was probably considerable. The severe repression of the activities of such men from time to time, under James I and Charles I, seems to have inclined some of them to opposition views. Perhaps there was a certain temperamental kinship

---

[1] *Special Passages and Certain Informations*, No. 24, Jan. 1642-3.

[2] Daniel Defoe, *A Tour through England and Wales*, Everyman edn, 1959, II, p. 86; Dymond, *op. cit.*, *passim*; N. J. Williams, *Tradesmen in Early-Stuart Wiltshire*, Wilts. Arch. and Nat. Hist. Soc., Records Branch, XV, 1960, pp. xiv–xv; Everitt, 'The Marketing of Agricultural Produce', in Thirsk, *op. cit.*, pp. 503–4, 559–62. For Northampton I have also relied on probate inventories and wills (Northants. Record Office), and on the Assembly Books, Freemen's Lists, etc. (Borough Records, Guildhall).

between their questing energy and the dynamism of the radical sects. An element of vehement puritanism in Northampton was directly connected with its importance as an entrepôt. Patchy though the evidence at present is, there are some indications of the way in which these wayfaring traders acquired and disseminated radical ideas.

Some Wealden cloth merchants, for example, regularly attended puritan sermons when they travelled to London to sell their cloth, and from thence returned with detailed notes of what they had heard to their home towns in Kent. In Elizabeth's reign the Familists are known to have spread their doctrines by going round the countryside as travelling basket-makers. Before the Civil War the Scottish Covenanters were said to be making use of wayfaring merchants "to convey intelligence and gain a party all over England." At Stourbridge Fair, near Cambridge, the greatest fair in the country, puritan preachers regularly discoursed to travelling traders gathered from distant parts. The inns of Cambridge itself had been used as centres for religious meetings since the days of the early Reformers. According to John Earle, writing in 1628, the carriers' inns and taverns of England were noted as centres for news and discussion. At Kidderminster Richard Baxter saw a distinct connexion between the puritan piety of the tradesmen of the town and their "constant converse and traffic with London" by way of the carrying trade. Not surprisingly, inns remained active centres of discussion throughout the Cromwellian period. An early Kentish Quaker, Luke Howard, recorded in the 1650s how he joined in a debate in an inn at Dover between Baptists, Brownists, Independents, and—at this period of their wilderness sojourn—episcopalians too.[1] It would be interesting to know what effects such meetings and debates had upon radicalism in the army; for both before and during the Civil War troops were billeted chiefly in the inns of provincial towns up and down the country, such as Dover, Canterbury, Bury St Edmunds, Ipswich, and Northampton.[2] They can hardly have remained unaffected by the puritan views of the travelling merchants they met there. Most probably, of course, the influence was a mutual one.

---

[1] *The Agricultural History Review*, XIV, 1966, p. 121; Ronald Knox, *Enthusiasm*, 1950, p. 171; John Nalson, *An Impartial Collection of the Great Affairs of State* . . ., 1682, I, p. 285; P. Collinson, *The Puritan Classical Movement in the Reign of Elizabeth I*, London Ph.D. thesis, 1957, p. 772n.; Sir John Neale, *Queen Elizabeth I*, Penguin edn, 1960, p. 189; John Earle, *Microcosmography*, 1920 edn, pp. 88, 90; Carl Bridenbaugh, *Vexed and Troubled Englishmen, 1590–1642*, 1968, p. 122 (quoting *Reliquiae Baxterianae*, I, p. 89); Madeline Jones, *op. cit.*, p. 485. For the reference to Earle I am indebted to Professor Carl Bridenbaugh. Dr Clive Holmes tells me that in Essex there are several presentations in the Church Court Act Books of drovers and wayfaring traders who spent their Sundays in travelling to market and neglected to attend their parish churches. Political pamphlets and 'libellous books' were also distributed in the market places where merchants met, for example at the time of the 1654 elections (Madeline Jones, *op. cit.*, p. 276n.).

[2] *Ibid.*, pp. 373, 375; Everitt, *Suffolk and the Great Rebellion*, p. 24.

The traditional association of the wayfaring community with the spread of sedition seems to have continued until the end of the seventeenth century. During times of crisis it tended to provoke vigorous reaction on the part of the government in an effort to suppress it. In May 1689, for example, a warrant was issued to Arthur Clum of the General Letter Office to search for treasonable and seditious printed libels, books, and papers about the persons and in the chambers and warehouses of all carriers, wagoners, packhorse-men, and hagglers on the western roads.[1]

The Professions and the Pseudo-Gentry

The period that saw the rise of the wayfaring community saw also, in the major provincial towns, a marked rise in the professional classes—lawyers, scriveners, physicians, surgeons, apothecaries, and schoolmasters. The increase of lawyers was no doubt partly due to the busy land-market of the time. It was also connected with the rapid expansion in dealing upon credit between 1570 and 1640. For this new kind of commercial transaction necessitated the drawing up of bipartite bonds and bills, by local lawyers or scriveners, and these instruments in turn helped to enrich the profession by frequently leading to legal disputes.[2] The growing need for an elementary business education in this context is shown by the publication of books like *A Complete Clerk and Scrivener's Guide*, issued in 1655. This volume contained "exact drafts and precedents of all manner of assurances and instruments now in use, as they were penned and perfected by divers learned judges, eminent lawyers, and great conveyancers."

The same need for business education is evident in the foundation of writing schools and similar educational establishments in the seventeenth and early eighteenth centuries. These were often somewhat fugitive affairs and are not easy to track down; but they are known to have existed in towns like Northampton from the middle years of the seventeenth century, if not before. John Conant, the vicar of All Saints' church in Northampton during the Protectorate, was in the habit of placing out poor children with local widows to learn to read, and then transferring the more promising pupils to writing schools in the town, "where he would keep them till they could write and cast accounts."[3] The extent of elementary education of this kind in the seventeenth century has perhaps been underestimated. In a recent study Joan Simon has gathered evidence for the existence of schoolmasters in at least 70 Leicestershire villages be-

[1] *Cal. State Papers Dom.*, 1689–90, p. 121. I owe this reference to Dr Joan Thirsk.

[2] Everitt, 'The Marketing of Agricultural Produce', in Thirsk, *op. cit.*, pp. 502, 555, 563–4. For the medical profession see R. S. Roberts, 'The Personnel and Practice of Medicine in Tudor and Stuart England', Pt. I, *Medical History*, VI, pp. 363–76.

[3] John Conant, *The Life of the Reverend and Venerable John Conant, D.D. . . . .*, 1823, pp. 79–80.

tween 1600 and 1640, besides 12 other foundations in market towns or with a settled endowment.[1] In Staffordshire, in the later seventeenth century, there may have been facilities for teaching poor boys and girls to write in perhaps half the parishes of the county. To judge from the signatures to their wills, about half the Staffordshire tradesmen of the time could read and write, and at least ten shops in the county are known to have stocked elementary school-books, such as primers, horn-books, and ABCs.[2]

In no town did the new professional classes of the provinces form more than a small fraction of the population. But their wealth, power, and prestige increased well beyond their mere rise in numbers. In Northampton the proportion of urban wealth in the hands of professional people, as recorded in probate inventories, rose from virtually nil in 1560–1600 to 10 per cent of that of all the people in the town between 1611 and 1640.[3] This may have been an exceptional increase; but there are signs of rapid growth generally, as Professor Notestein and others have suggested. In Norwich, for example, those engaged in professions more than trebled in numbers between 1525 and 1575. In the seventeenth century there was certainly an important group of local legal families in busy county towns like Preston and Maidstone. Even in quite a modest shire-centre, such as Stafford, there was usually a substantial number of surgeons and apothecaries. In the cathedral city of Canterbury there were no fewer than 22 medical doctors between 1603 and 1643.[4] There was evidently comfortable dying, as well as comfortable living, under the shadow of the Primate of All England.

In their upper ranks these new professional families in provincial towns merged into what I have ventured to call elsewhere the 'pseudo-gentry': that class of leisured and predominantly urban families who, by their manner of life, were commonly regarded as gentry, though they were not supported by a landed estate.[5] In most areas these pseudo-gentry began to emerge into prominence in the latter half of the seventeenth century; but their origins can sometimes be traced back in towns like Preston, Canterbury, and Northampton to the period before the Civil War. Some of them stemmed from junior

[1] Brian Simon, ed., *Education in Leicestershire, 1540–1940*, 1968, chapter 1 (by Joan Simon), p. 21, and Appendix I.

[2] *Ex inf.* Miss Marie Rowlands.

[3] The original inventories for Northampton do not survive for these years; but their valuations are endorsed on the wills, and these provide the basis for the percentages given in the text.

[4] Wallace Notestein, *The English People on the Eve of Colonization, 1603–1630*, 1954, pp. 93–5; J. F. Pound, 'The Social and Trade Structure of Norwich, 1525–1575', *Past and Present*, No. 34, July 1966, p. 60; Defoe, *op. cit.*, II, p. 268; *ex inf.* Miss Marie Rowlands; John H. Raach, *A Directory of English Country Physicians, 1603–43*, 1962, pp. 105, 106.

[5] Everitt, 'Social Mobility in Early Modern England', *Past and Present*, No. 33, April 1966, pp. 70–2.

branches of local landed gentry; others from the legal, medical, and clerical families of provincial towns. Characteristically they lacked the deep local roots of either the older gentry of the countryside or the genuine trading dynasties of the towns. They migrated more readily from place to place, and in consequence played an important part in disseminating the new tastes and manners of the time. As their wills and probate inventories reveal, their demands in matters of domestic comfort helped to refine the standards of contemporary taste and craftsmanship in the provinces. In the rebuilding of towns like Warwick and Northampton on a more regular plan in the late seventeenth century, their influence was probably considerable.[1] In the eighteenth century they played a prominent part in the founding of new social institutions, such as the county infirmaries established in towns like Northampton and Worcester.

One of the interesting facts about the new professional groups of the seventeenth century is that, as the period of the Great Rebellion progressed, they came to form one of the dominant elements, sometimes the predominant one, in the parliamentarian county committees. This was not necessarily because they specifically set out to oust the country gentry from their inherited position as local governors. It was partly because the county families themselves seceded from their support of parliament, and because somebody had to be found to do their administrative work. It was also partly because very large committees, of up to 50 or 60 members, were notoriously inefficient. Cromwell was determined to increase the efficiency of the county committees by reducing their active membership and by exerting control over them through their usually more amenable members—these professional men. The increase in professional power also occurred because, as committee business became more burdensome, more involved in technical and legal problems, only local lawyers and the like were able to unravel its complexities.[2]

The same increase in professional power during the 1650s is also evident in the affairs of the municipal corporations. Many towns at this time returned local lawyers or other professional people to parliament, instead of the country gentry they had usually elected hitherto. Prominent in the affairs of Maidstone, for instance, throughout 1642–60, were Andrew Broughton, a very able local lawyer who later became a regicide, and John Banks, a wealthy scrivener who formed a kind of estate agency in the town. Prominent at Dover were Thomas Day, a local surgeon, and John Golder, one of the town's physicians. At Canter-

[1] For the kind of tastes characteristic of the pseudo-gentry cf. the descriptions of provincial towns in: Defoe, *op. cit.*, II, pp. 84, 86, 91, 268 (Warwick, Northampton, Newark, Lincoln, Preston); *The Journeys of Celia Fiennes*, ed. Christopher Morris, 1949, pp. 118, 164, 187 (Northampton, Tamworth, Preston); *The Diary of John Evelyn*, ed. William Bray, Everyman edn, 1952, I, pp. 282, 300 (Northampton, Leicester).

[2] Madeline Jones, *op. cit.*, pp. 258–9; Everitt, *Community of Kent*, pp. 151–2 and n., 286–97.

bury the leading part in the 1650s was taken by two very astute and unscrupulous local lawyers, Thomas St Nicholas and Vincent Denne, who also represented the city in parliament. At Rochester John Parker, the recorder, and Peter Pett and Richard Hutchinson, two professional men from the dockyard, kept the city in submission to the new régime. Most influential of all the professional people in Kent during the Great Rebellion were Lambarde Godfrey, another Maidstone lawyer, who became the solicitor for sequestrations to the county committee, and Charles Bowles, who had been trained in Chatham dockyard, and became the committee's commissary and accountant. Between them, these two men controlled the whole of the taxation of the shire, and scores of thousands of acres of sequestrated royalist and ecclesiastical land. At no time before, and perhaps not again till after the foundation of county councils in Queen Victoria's reign, did professional people wield such power in provincial society.[1]

Yet in the last resort the power of these professional men was more limited than it seemed. In the seventeenth century the power of all rulers, whether kings, peers, judges, bishops, major-generals, or justices of the peace, was limited. It was bounded not simply or mainly by the law, but by the density, the intractability, of provincial life. How immensely vital, how marvellously obstinate the little local worlds of seventeenth-century England often were! How indestructible! They had to be, of course, or they would never have survived. By 1660 they had been learning to be so for the past 600 years. When one reads of how the little towns of Stuart Kent, none of them save Canterbury with more than 3,000 people, defied every successive government's attempt to reform their corporations, defied the whole might of Charles I, of parliament, and of Cromwell by every legal device and personal subterfuge in their power, and still emerged unvanquished, almost unchanged, one cannot refrain from a certain wonder and admiration. They could teach the modern provincial cities something, and maybe the universities too, about their relationship with Westminster.

IV THE PROVINCES AND THE NATION

IN one of the illuminating asides which sometimes made his articles suggestive, S. R. Gardiner once referred to that important part of the English nation which felt satisfied with neither side in the Great Rebellion, yet could not embody its own ideals in any practicable policy.[2] It is tempting to

---

[1] *Ibid.*, pp. 151–2 and n., 179, 290 and n., and chapter v, *passim*; Madeline Jones, *op. cit.*, pp. 257–9, 304.

[2] *D.N.B.*, *sub* Sir Edward Dering.

identify this mass of dissatisfied Englishmen with the native and provincial world with which this paper has been concerned. Though the identification would in some ways be misleading, it contains more than an element of truth. For though the intractability of the provincial world in a certain sense defeated both Charles I and the Commonwealth, under neither régime did the provinces formulate their ideals in any practicable or coherent policy. They could not do so because, in the nature of things, their society was dispersed and their ideals almost infinitely varied. They had no single capital to focus their loyalties; for London drew to itself only certain threads in their life. Instead they had many centres; they consisted of many worlds, each living out its own half-separate life, largely unaware of the ways of thought of other regions. In time of supreme emergency, as in 1640 or 1660, these communities were capable of united action on particular issues, largely through the instrumentality of the gentry. But when the crisis passed, the unity itself dissolved; for even the gentry, for the most part, were still essentially provincial people.

The fact that the great mass of provincial Englishmen never embodied their ideals in a single, coherent policy has perpetuated, if it did not originate, a distortion in the popular image of the Great Rebellion. Cavalier or Roundhead, Royalist or Parliamentarian: these are still the categories into which, subconsciously, the layman divides the country and its inhabitants between 1640 and 1660. But most people were probably neither the one nor the other. They supported parliament in 1640 and the monarchy in 1660, or so it seemed. But they did so without necessarily involving themselves in any very deep sympathy with either.[1] For the fact was, as already remarked, that for the most part they were simply not concerned with affairs of state. They only became involved in them when the gyrations of politicians became more than ordinarily demented, and threatened the structure of their own local and largely self-centred world as a consequence.

One of the basic problems throughout the Great Rebellion was the unresolved tension between the provincial's loyalty to his local world and his loyalty to the state. This tension arose because the era which had seen the rise of the nation-state had also seen a parallel rise in provincial self-consciousness. Not that either phenomenon was altogether new. Though there had not always been an England, there had been one for many centuries, and there had been local communities—villages, towns, and counties—for a still longer period. Still, the growth of the sense of identity and independence, under the Tudors and Stuarts, is evident in both the national and the local sphere. Until recent

[1] This was probably true of most people even in reputedly puritan areas like Northamptonshire and Buckinghamshire, which veered strongly towards the king's side after the fall of Leicester in May 1645.—Cf. H. G. Tibbutt, ed., *The Letter Books of Sir Samuel Luke, 1644–45,* 1963, pp. 292, 304.

years it has not been so well attested in the latter as in the former; but through the work of A. L. Rowse, Mary Coate, T. G. Barnes, and other scholars we are now well aware of its existence in the county communities of England. Even today, however, we are insufficiently conscious of its vitality in the urban and village communities of the period.

There were many reasons for this growing sense of provincial self-consciousness during the sixteenth and seventeenth centuries. It emerged with the growing power of the county commonwealths of England. It emerged with the rise of the county capitals, focusing as they did so many aspects of the shire communities around them. It developed, too, with the rise of the professional classes, called into being to serve the new needs of both town and countryside. It arose with the expansion of trade and wealth generally, for this expansion greatly increased the wealth of provincial townsmen and yeomen. Indeed, it was one of the ironies of provincial life that even the revolutionary developments of the time, such as the rise of the new gentry and the emergence of the wayfaring community, in the end came to be accepted and naturalized within it and to buttress its independence. The new developments were grafted into the old tree, so to speak, rejuvenating and invigorating its productive powers without fundamentally altering its identity. In a real sense the events of 1660 were a compromise between the power of this provincial world and the power of the nation-state. Or rather they were an agreement to differ, an *entente*, a recognition that each world needed the other in order to survive. But the two worlds went on: connected, it is true, but in their origins and their sources of life still in many respects unrelated.

By 1660 or 1700 there were undeniably a number of profound changes at work within the body of provincial life. Amongst the most important were a certain hardening of class distinctions in the latter half of the seventeenth century, and a gradual orientation of the topmost level of society, the greater gentry, towards national and metropolitan ways of thought. The processes were gradual, very gradual, and they did not affect all parts or all people equally. They were nowhere complete; but their existence in most parts of England is difficult to deny. During the 1640s two significant words became current in the English language, and both point to the change. The phrase 'the Quality' came into common use to describe the gentry, and to mark them off as a separate caste, almost a separate race, from the rest of the people. The other, the word 'fleering', was an epithet applied by the unprivileged to that unpleasant phenomenon, the contempt of the Oxford Cavaliers for their social inferiors.[1] It would be very naïve to suppose that the attitudes implicit in these

---

[1] The *Oxford English Dictionary* ascribes the two words, used in these senses, to the late seventeenth century. But they occur in some of the Thomason Tracts with these meanings by 1648. Phrases like

phrases were absent from English society before 1640, or that they rapidly became universal thereafter. But when two such words, closely related in meaning, catch on at the same time, it seems to indicate a shift of emphasis in contemporary society, a certain change in the unspoken assumptions of the age.

How did this shift of emphasis arise, and why did it persist? Only a few of the many reasons for its development need be singled out here. One was the fact that during the Civil War many gentry were cut off from their local roots, and forced to rub shoulders with men of all ranks and classes in the crowded streets of Oxford and other garrison towns. Divorced from their local duties and their local power, the older men were driven to bolster their position by rigid class-assertion, and the younger Cavaliers by a kind of senseless personal pride that often made them unpopular with ordinary folk. "Lofty, desperate, and discontented-minded spirits": so the people of Kent described the Cavaliers who came into the county to join the Rising of 1648.[1] The situation seems to have been aggravated by the remarkable surplus of landless younger sons in the king's armies, with no estate to root them in the countryside, no career but the army open to them, and little to support their pretensions to gentility but the way they dressed and spoke, and the arrogance of their bearing. The more stay-at-home and old-fashioned people of their own degree, like Sir Roger Twysden and Sir George Sondes, they ridiculed, as "the female gentry of the smock."[2] Their own sometimes rather tragic sense of insecurity and uncertainty they sublimated in extravagant notions of 'honour', and in a sort of pseudo-religious worship of Charles I and Henrietta Maria.

The changing caste-sense of the time was not confined to the Cavaliers alone, however. In the general shake-up of social classes during the Great Rebellion it became equally remarkable amongst some of the doctrinaire puritans. In Kent, says Dr Madeline Jones, puritan clergy "for the most part . . . despised the unredeemed and irredeemable mob." They made little attempt to civilize them, and rarely fell into the error of identifying poverty with virtue. As John Crompe, the minister of All Saints, Maidstone, once observed, "many are very poor, and very profane", and only on rare occasions does God choose "very obscure and contemptible persons."[3] John Crompe himself, significantly enough, came of a minor armigerous family in the county: and his sentiments would probably have been echoed by puritans of similar status in other parts of the country. Was there ever a more arrant snob, for instance, than Mrs Lucy Hutchinson, or Sir Simonds D'Ewes? Perhaps to the peculiar puritan cast of

'gentleman of quality' occur by the early seventeenth century; but there seems to me a slight but significant difference of emphasis in the phrase 'the Quality', used to identify the gentry as a distinct caste.

[1] Quoted in Everitt, *Community of Kent*, p. 252.
[2] The phrase occurs in B.M., Harleian MS 6918, f. 34.   [3] Madeline Jones, *op. cit.*, pp. 460, 467.

mind which found pleasure in procrustean theological systems and quibbling legal formulae, the current forms of human society inevitably came to be regarded as a part of the eternal order. It is noteworthy that the same attitude emerged once again amongst the spiritual descendants of the puritan gentry, the upper-class evangelicals of the nineteenth century, most implacable of all opponents of democratic equality.

With the end of the Civil War and the return of the Cavaliers to their native communities, this sudden hardening of class distinctions might have been expected to ease up again. But for a variety of reasons little relaxation took place. Amongst some of the Cavalier gentry, the enforced absenteeism of the war bred a restless temperament, and they could not settle down again to the ordinary routine of country life. Their divorce from the local community became a permanent fact of their existence. Some prosperous squires like the Tokes of Godinton in Kent, whose grandfathers had husbanded the family estates with so much care and interest in the time of James I, now ceased to farm their lands themselves and became mere *rentiers*, migrating from London to Bath, and from Bath to Tunbridge Wells, as the whim took them. The rising spas of the time, like Tunbridge Wells, owed much of their prosperity to the spendthrift manner of life of these Cavaliers. They did not all become absentees, but their manor houses often ceased to be farmhouses, and became instead mere gentlemen's seats, shut off behind walls and palings from the inquisitive eyes of vulgar persons.

Lower down in the scale, amongst the minor gentry, those who did not succeed in extending their property by judicious speculation in the marriage market, sometimes sank to the humdrum level of yeomen-farmers. The very large number of rural manor houses in counties like Devon, Norfolk, Lincolnshire, and Kent which, by Queen Victoria's time, had become no more than farmhouses bears witness to the remarkable decrease in the numbers of minor gentry between the Restoration and 1800.[1] The decay of one such house at Haslingfield (Cambridgeshire) prompted Viscount Torrington, on one of his journeys in 1790, to deplore "in my old style the desertion of the country by the gentlemen and good yeomanry. An hundred years ago every village afforded two good gentlemen's houses; and within these 60 years the hall or the court still remained." But now "the old mansion being deserted, and no longer the seat of hospitality and the resort of sportsmen, is left to tumble down . . . The

---

[1] Everitt, *Community of Kent*, pp. 326–7; 'Social Mobility in Early Modern England', pp. 64–7 and n.; S. Baring-Gould, *Old Country Life*, 1890, chapter I. The decline of hundreds of manor houses in Kent to the status of farms seems to have taken place chiefly in the period from about 1680 to 1820. I am hoping to publish shortly a paper on the buildings of Kent, analysing the 15,000 buildings in the county dating from before c. 1830 and the 5,000 from before c. 1640, in which this theme, amongst others, will be elaborated.

poor cottagers, who are soon reduced to half their former number, are con-
signed over to the few farmers; and nothing remains of the old hall but some
tottering walls and uncultivated kitchen gardens." Torrington, no doubt, was
a reactionary, and his explanation of the decay was coloured by sentiment; but
his remarks were not entirely without foundation, as others have observed.[1]

The subject is one which would repay much more detailed local investiga-
tion, both in documents and on the ground, than it has yet received.[2] Few
buildings are more evocative today of a vanished world than the ruined manor-
houses of Norfolk, their chimneys overgrown with ivy, their gardens a pathetic
wilderness of nettles and willowherb. Local in origin, local in plan, local in
style, they grew up over the years, as each generation extended or altered the
old family home. Their decay is more than the decay of a kind of building: it
is the decay of a civilization—the old provincial civilization of the richest
county in England.

Yet the changes of the Restoration period should not be over-emphasized.
Probably they did not immediately affect more than a minority of people,
even amongst the armigerous classes. In 1660 the old provincial world still had
another two centuries of life before it, and for many towns these years included
the golden generations between 1680 and 1820. Everywhere, it is true, the new
fashions of metropolitan England gradually came to be adopted; but in the
process of adoption they underwent a subtle metamorphosis, a surprising
naturalization to their new habitat. The provincial root-stock imparted its own
peculiar vigour, its own rough energy, to the ideals of the time. Local archi-
tecture blossomed into fresh vitality; the standards of taste and skill were transformed; the numbers of specialized craftsmen doubled or trebled in the older
county towns like Northampton.

Such was the strength of this old provincial society of England that it survived in full vigour till the early years of the nineteenth century, slowly changing with the times, but unchanging in its essential personality. In many parts
it continued to exist, alongside the new industrial civilization, till the eve of the
First World War. Like all human societies it had its shortcomings. Yet it was
after all the civilization that shaped the minds of some of the ablest English-

[1] *The Torrington Diaries*, ed. C. B. Andrews, II, 1935, pp. 237–8.

[2] For general discussions of the growth of the greater landed estates and the decline of the smaller,
see G. E. Mingay, *English Landed Society in the Eighteenth Century*, 1963, chapters II–IV; F. M. L. Thomp-
son, 'The Social Distribution of Landed Property in England since the Sixteenth Century', *Econ. Hist.
Rev.*, 2nd Ser., XIX, No. 3, Dec. 1966, pp. 505–17. Professor Mingay's conclusion, based on scattered
examples in different counties, is that this tendency lasted from the late seventeenth to the mid-
eighteenth century (p. 50). While in no way dissenting from his balanced and judicious analysis, I
believe it is also essential to study the community of gentry *as a whole* in a particular county, over this
period, and to study the evidence of surviving buildings and their history along with the documents.

men. It was the world of many of the great Victorian novelists, and it was the one whose ways of thought they described, with marvellous insight, in some of their finest novels. And certainly it was no contemptible civilization that gave birth to a series of books like *The Chronicles of Carlingford*, and bequeathed to mankind a masterpiece so moving as *Middlemarch*, or a history so profound as *The Old Wives' Tale*.[1]

[1] *Middlemarch*, *Adam Bede*, and *The Mill on the Floss* are based on provincial life in and around Coventry, Nuneaton, and Gainsborough. Margaret Oliphant's Carlingford is not precisely identifiable, but from internal evidence it was clearly a small town in southern England or possibly the south Midlands. The best of the five full-scale novels devoted to Carlingford are *Salem Chapel*, *Miss Marjoribanks*, and *Phoebe Junior*. Strictly speaking Margaret Oliphant's original background was not the provincial civilization of England. How she acquired her intimate knowledge of it is something of a mystery. She was born in Scotland, lived for most of her girlhood in Liverpool, married a cousin living in London, and after his early death, apart from visits abroad, spent the rest of her life at Windsor. But her insight into many aspects of the older provincial life is of great value to the historian. The best of her work certainly stands comparison with Trollope or Mrs Gaskell. (Cf. Robert and Vineta Colby, *The Equivocal Virtue: Mrs Oliphant and the Victorian Literary Market Place*, 1966, p. xiv.)

APPENDIX

THE DISTRIBUTION OF WEALTH IN ENGLAND

Table I The Monthly Assessments, 1648–60[1]

1 Date of assessment	2 Monthly total assessed on England & Wales	3 Norfolk	4 Suffolk	5 Kent	6 Essex	7 London	8 Devon	9 Yorkshire	10 Westminster and Middlesex	11 Leicestershire and Northants.	12 Total of columns 3–9[3]
17 Mar. 1648[2]	£60,000	£5,010 =8·3%	£4,763 =7·9%	£4,763 =7·9%	£4,547 =7·6%	£3,908 =6·5%	£3,655 =6·1%	£2,312 =3·9%	£1,522 =2·5%	£1,059 =1·8%	£28,958 =48·2%
7 Dec. 1649	£90,000	£4,900 =5·4%	£4,700 =5·2%	£4,700 =5·2%	£4,500 =5·0%	£6,000 =6·7%	£4,000 =4·4%	£4,000 =4·4%	£2,300 =2·6%	£3,200 =3·6%	£32,800 =36·4%
10 Dec. 1652	£120,000	£6,533 =5·4%	£6,267 =5·2%	£6,267 =5·2%	£6,000 =5·0%	£8,000 =6·7%	£5,333 =4·4%	£5,333 =4·4%	£3,067 =2·6%	£4,267 =3·6%	£43,733 =36·4%
8 June 1654	£90,000	£4,890 =5·3%	£4,700 =5·2%	£4,700 =5·2%	£4,500 =5·0%	£6,000 =6·7%	£4,000 =4·4%	£4,000 =4·4%	£2,300 =2·6%	£3,200 =3·6%	£32,790 =36·4%
26 Jan. 1660	£70,000	£3,811 =5·4%	£3,656 =5·2%	£3,656 =5·2%	£3,500 =5·0%	£4,667 =6·7%	£3,111 =4·4%	£3,111 =4·4%	£1,789 =2·6%	£2,489 =3·6%	£25,512 =36·4%

NOTES:

[1] The counties are listed according to their proportion of the total burden of the assessment of 17 March 1648. Those listed in columns 3–9 (including London) were the seven most heavily assessed in England throughout this period. The counties in columns 10 and 11 (with Westminster) were not the next most heavily burdened to Yorkshire, but are included for comparative purposes. The figures in the Table are taken from the original ordinances printed in C. H. Firth and R. S. Rait, *Acts and Ordinances of the Interregnum, 1642–1660*, 1911. They are given here to the nearest pound.

[2] The ordinances fixing the monthly assessments before 1648 do not cover the whole country, so that it is impossible to calculate valid figures before that date. That of 21 February 1645, for example, covers only 26 counties, and excludes Wales and the south-west.

[3] From the spring of 1648 till the autumn of 1649 the four most heavily burdened counties of Norfolk, Suffolk, Kent, and Essex each paid considerably more in assessments than London, and their total taxation amounted to nearly one-third of that of all England and Wales (31·7 per cent). From December 1649 to January 1660 their assessments were reduced by nearly 11 per cent, to 20·8 per cent of the total for England and Wales. The reduction was met by raising the assessments of several Midland and northern counties, which had probably till then been under-assessed. The assessments for Leicestershire and Northamptonshire, it will be noted, were doubled from December 1649.

Table II   The Hearth Tax Assessments, 1662[1]

	Hearths	Percentage of all hearths	Acreage	Acres per hearth[2]
I: 0–15 acres per hearth				
1. London, including Westminster and Southwark	156,361	9·7	4,295	0·03
2. Middlesex, excluding London and Westminster	94,508	5·9	177,316	2
3. Surrey	47,583	2·9	485,120	10
4. Kent[3]	79,532	5·0	995,015	12
5. Suffolk	64,131	4·0	948,269	15
6. Essex	63,833	4·0	979,532	15
7. Oxfordshire	31,379	1·9	479,220	15
8. Hertfordshire	27,172	1·7	404,523	15
Total	564,499	34·9	4,473,290	14[4]
II: 16–20 acres per hearth				
9. Berkshire	28,347	1·8	463,830	16
10. Somerset, excluding Bristol	62,064	3·8	1,037,594	17
11. Gloucestershire, including Bristol	45,053	2·8	805,842	18
12. Worcestershire	25,138	1·5	458,352	18
13. Norfolk	73,911	4·6	1,315,064	18
14. Bedfordshire	16,990	1·0	302,942	18
15. Buckinghamshire	25,055	1·5	479,360	19
16. Cambridgeshire	27,447	1·7	553,241	20
17. Huntingdonshire	11,986	0·7	233,985	20
Total	315,991	19·5	5,650,210	18
III: 21–25 acres per hearth				
18. Devon	77,794	4·8	1,671,364	21
19. Northamptonshire	30,398	1·9	638,612	21
20. Sussex[3]	42,880	2·6	932,471	22
21. Wiltshire	39,121	2·4	864,101	22
22. Dorset	28,416	1·8	625,612	22
23. Warwickshire	27,116	1·7	605,275	22
24. Rutland	4,228	0·2	97,273	23
25. Hampshire	44,640	2·8	1,053,042	24
26. Leicestershire	21,934	1·3	532,779	24
Total	316,527	19·6	7,020,529	22

NOTES:

[1] The numbers of hearths are taken from *Dorset Hearth Tax Assessments, 1662–1664*, ed. C. A. F. Meekings, 1951, pp. 108–10. Acreages relate to county areas before modern boundary alterations.

[2] Except in the case of London the figures are given to the nearest acre.

[3] The figures for Kent and Sussex are approximate, since the Cinque Ports were separately assessed at 12,504 hearths. The five largest ports and their 'limbs' (Dover, Sandwich, Faversham, Deal, and Tenterden) were all in Kent, and accounted for 7,163 hearths. The remaining places reckoned with the Kentish ports probably brought the total to about 9,000. I have added this figure to Kent and 3,504 to Sussex.

[4] Excluding London and Middlesex.

		Hearths	Percentage of all hearths	Acreage	Acres per hearth
	IV: 26–35 acres per hearth				
27.	Cheshire	24,867	1·5	657,950	26
28.	Cornwall	32,046	2·0	868,167	27
29.	Staffordshire	27,226	1·7	741,318	27
30.	Lancashire	43,496	2·7	1,194,555	27
31.	Nottinghamshire	19,032	1·2	540,123	28
32.	Shropshire	29,134	1·8	861,800	30
33.	Derbyshire	20,964	1·3	650,369	31
34.	Herefordshire	17,514	1·1	538,924	31
35.	Yorkshire	111,211	6·9	3,889,432	35
	Total	325,490	20·1	9,942,638	31
	V: More than 35 acres per hearth				
36.	Lincolnshire	47,891	3·0	1,705,293	36
37.	Durham	17,624	1·1	649,244	37
38.	Westmorland	6,095	0·4	504,917	83
39.	Northumberland	14,786	0·9	1,291,515	87
40.	Cumberland	9,372	0·6	973,086	104
	Total	95,768	5·9	5,124,055	54

Table III (a)   The Wealth of Yorkshire Families, c. 1640

	All families	Peers[1]	Baronets[2]	Knights[2]	Squires & Gentlemen[2]
Numbers	691	12	28	62	589[3]
Total wealth	£315,800	£45,800	£43,000	£68,000	£159,000
Percentage of total wealth	100	15	14	22	50
Average wealth	£457	£3,817	£1,536	£1,097	£270

Table III (b)   The Wealth of Kentish Families, c. 1640[4]

	All families	Peers	Baronets	Knights	Squires & Gentlemen
Numbers	841	10	31	50	750[3]
Total wealth	£330,595	£40,890	£43,555	£43,650	£202,500
Percentage of total wealth	100	12	13	13	61
Average wealth	£393	£4,089	£1,405	£873	£270

NOTES:

[1] The 12 Yorkshire peers and their incomes were: Cumberland (£5,500), Wharton (£5,500), Mulgrave (£3,300), Eure (£3,000), Strafford (£6,000+), Fauconberg (£3,000), Savile (£3,800), Darcy of Hornby (£3,500), Darcy of Aston (£4,000), Fairfax of Gilling (£2,700), Cameron (Fairfax of Denton), (c. £2,500), and Dunbar (£3,000). For Fauconberg, Savile, Darcy of Hornby, Darcy of Aston, Eure, Fairfax of Gilling, Cameron, Strafford, and Dunbar I have relied on information from Dr J. T. Cliffe; and for the remainder on Professor Stone's figures of rentals in 1641 (*The Crisis of the*

Aristocracy, 1558–1641, 1965, p. 761). In utilizing the latter I have taken the mean figure of the rental category to which each peer is allotted. The precise figure for each peer is not given in Professor Stone's table.

[2] These calculations are based on information of family incomes generously supplied by Dr J. T. Cliffe.

[3] The problem of defining the 'gentry', in their lowest ranks, is considerable, and more so in some counties than others. In Kent I have included all who are known to have been armigerous, and a number who, while their right to arms is now difficult to prove, were widely reckoned as gentry at the time and usually intermarried with other armigerous families. It may well be that I have included some families whose north-country equivalents would not be included in the Yorkshire figures given above. In a personal note Dr Cliffe tells me that if he had included "men who styled themselves 'gentry' without due authority the total would undoubtedly be in excess of 1,000." But he has quite properly included in his figures only those who were genuinely armigerous, and for Yorkshire I have felt it safer to follow his example. It would in fact be difficult to make any adjustment in the comparative figures (if such an adjustment is necessary) because of differences in the local structure of society in the two counties. In Kent and some other counties (for example Devon and Leicestershire) there was not a sharp distinction in status or manner of life between the very small gentry and the richer yeomen. In some shires, on the other hand—for example Northamptonshire—the distinction seems to have been more strictly observed.

[4] This table is not based on a complete survey for all 841 gentry, but on a sample of 135 families (cf. my *Community of Kent*, p. 329). For further comments upon the subject see my review article 'The Peers and the Provinces', *The Agricultural History Review*, xvi, i, 1968, pp. 60–7.